Alexander Emerson Belcher

**What I Know about Commercial Travelling**

Who we Are; what we Do, and how we Do it

Alexander Emerson Belcher

**What I Know about Commercial Travelling**
*Who we Are; what we Do, and how we Do it*

ISBN/EAN: 9783337205379

Printed in Europe, USA, Canada, Australia, Japan

Cover: Foto ©Lupo / pixelio.de

More available books at **www.hansebooks.com**

Heartily yours.
Alex. Emerson. Belcher,

# KNOW ABOUT COMMERCIAL TRAVELLING.

## WHO WE ARE; WHAT WE DO,

### AND

## HOW WE DO IT.

BY

A. EMERSON BELCHER.

Toronto:
HUNTER, ROSE & CO., 25 WELLINGTON ST. WEST.
1883.

Entered according to the Act of the Parliament of Canada, in the year one thousand eight hundred and eighty-three, by A. EMERSON BELCHER, in the Office of the Minister of Agriculture.

I MOST RESPECTFULLY

## Dedicate

THESE UNPRETENDING IDEAS OF COMMERCIAL LIFE

TO MY

## FELLOW COMMERCIALS,

WHO I HAVE FOUND TO BE A CLASS OF

INTELLIGENT, COURTEOUS, OBLIGING & COMMUNICATIVE

## Gentlemen,

AMONG WHOM I HAVE SPENT SOME OF THE MOST AGREEABLE AND PLEASANT HOURS OF MY LIFE.

WITH BEST WISHES TO ALL,

A. EMERSON BELCHER.

# PREFACE.

THE author, in presenting this book to the public and the "Craft," hopes to provoke discussion by it concerning our "life on the road," by which means existing evils may be remedied, and improvements brought about.

While not claiming the work to be official, and admitting that it may contain errors, it is, nevertheless, the honest opinions and convictions of fourteen years' experience.

In dealing with the different subjects, he has endeavoured to give credit where credit is due, and to apply the lash where it was needed. Hoping for a lenient criticism, and that some one in the future may improve upon it, he sends it forth to do its work.

# CONTENTS.

## CHAPTER I.

### THE DIFFERENT KINDS OF COMMERCIAL TRAVELLERS.

PAGE

Who we are—The Heavy Commercial—The Polite—The Noble—The Green—The Eccentric—The Nervous—The Lazy—The Antiquated—The Persevering—The Spreeing—The Religious—The Industrious Successful........................................................ 9

## CHAPTER II.

### WHAT A COMMERCIAL TRAVELLER SHOULD BE.

What a traveller should be—Good Appearance—Good Manners—Good Natured—Eloquent—Enthusiastic—Pluck—Endurance—Self Reliance—Punctuality—Diligence—A Little Assurance—Truthful—Decision—Energy—Caution—Policy—Perseverance—Attention to detail—Quickness and Rapidity—Steadiness—Honorable—Good judge of character—Self Respect—Able to pocket Affronts—Must Excel—Loving and Religious.................................. 65

## CHAPTER III.

### OUR CUSTOMERS.

Our Customers—The Model Polite A 1 Customer—The Civil, Jolly Customer—The Punctual, Industrious and Successful Customer—The Advertising, Go-ahead Customer—The Careful, Prudent, Cautious Customer—The Systematic Customer—The Fault-finding, Unpunctual Customer—The Incautious, Talkative Customer—The Too-knowing Customer—The Fast Customer—The Fossilized Customer—The Impudent, Bull-dog, Know-nothing Customer—Customers who are so on Sufrage...................................... 98

## CHAPTER IV.

### OUR EMPLOYERS.

PAGE

Our Employers—A word of advice to our Employers—Employers exercising Policy .................................................. 120

## CHAPTER V.

### THE HOTELS.

The Hotels—Our Homes when away from Home—The Home-like, Good Hotel—The Pretty Fair Hotel—The Very Indifferent Hotel—The Decidedly Bad Hotel .................................. 130

## CHAPTER VI.

### THE RAILROADS.

Concerning Conductors ............................................. 139

## CHAPTER VII.

Conclusion ........................................................ 145

# WHAT I KNOW ABOUT COMMERCIAL TRAVELLING.

## CHAPTER I.

### THE DIFFERENT KINDS OF COMMERCIAL TRAVELLERS.

Who we are—The Heavy Commercial—The Polite—The Noble—The Green—The Eccentric—The Nervous—The Lazy—The Antiquated—The Persevering—The Spreeing—The Religious—The Industrious Successful.

"HARRISBURG! Harrisburg! change cars here for Brantford and the Wellington, Grey & Bruce branch," greeted our ears from the sonorous voice of the brakeman on the train upon which we were a passenger. A general bustle of people about to leave the train takes place. Fathers gathering together their children, and the mothers adjusting their hats, etc., on the little things; young ladies relieving the car racks of sundry little articles, together with the inevitable band-box that usually occupies the other half of the seat with them; old men adjusting their great coats; and the old lady, who is perhaps alone, and on her way to visit friends, seizes the

A

old hemp carpet bag, which has done **duty in** this capacity **every** time any member of **the** family has any travelling **to do,** and the old gingham umbrella, which she **gathers under** her arm, **and manages, on her** way through the car, **to** poke a **good many people in** the ribs **with,** as she struggles to reach the door, long before the train stops. A **good** number are standing and balancing themselves to keep **their** feet as the train is being brought **to** a standstill. When will people learn to keep their seats until the train stops.

A few of the passengers are notable exceptions, they *do* **keep their** seats, and with satchels, **coats,** parcels, etc., usually manage to occupy what would seat two or three persons. In these individuals the initiated will recognise "the only," "**the** original," "**the** commercial traveller." The writer making one **of** the happy number, we pick up our traps, and with the rest **soon find** ourselves **upon the** platform. The first face that our eyes catch is **our** old friend Ansley, **in** the **hat line.** It always does one good to meet a man of Alf's stamp; would there were more like him! We rushed up to him with the "Hallo, old fellow, how are you and your Canada straws prospering?" "Oh, immense, never had a better trip thus far. Our goods are right (any house Alf represents, the goods and house must be right,) and the merchants know it. Business is better with customers, and they are all glad to see us, even with Canada straws in December. Well, where have you been and where are you going?" "Going to Brantford; which way are you going?" "I am with you." We are here interrupted in our pleasant chat by the conductor calling, "all aboard for Brantford—across the other side of the track for Brantford!" We move across, and in getting in, encounter again the old lady of the hemp carpet bag and umbrella. We come to the rescue, and help the old lady up the slippery steps, not forgetting to relieve her of the umbrella, knowing how people value their eyes, and not knowing what mischief she might do if left to wield it herself. After all become seated, we glance around us as usual, and take in the faces of those who are our fellow passengers. Besides the old lady and some others on business or pleasure bent, there were a number of commercial travellers, for what train can you board without finding more or less of these gentry. Not only will you find them on trains, but steamboats, stages and private traps, and if you were to visit the remotest part of our civilization in a new country where villages spring up as if by magic, some one has put up a clap-board structure, and put out a shingle with "general store" upon it. Chance to drop in there, and you will find the Commercial Traveller with his samples pushing for an order. It is said that

> Commercial travellers will find their way
> Where wolves won't dare to stray.

The Commercials of this country have become an institution, both strong and influential, and comprise among their number a diversity of genius and character, such as is seldom met with in any other class of the community. As they are the pick or cream of the employees, they are selected from among the many to fill the important position of representing large commercial institutions, among the business men of the cities, towns and villages of this fine growing country.

This is an important position, as the men selected carry with them the credentials of their firms, and the firm is often judged by the bearing, respectability and integrity of the traveller. So you will see why it is that the best are picked, and I may say here that employees cannot be too particular in their selections. The great aim of the "Boys" in the warehouse is to get on the road, perhaps their desires are heightened by the wonderful yarns that our "returned commercial" is enabled to spin to them of his experiences "last trip." They are led to believe that the life is all sunshine and that we are having a good time at our employers' expense, forgetting that,

"Every sunshine has its shadow."

However, the position commands better pay, and to the recruit the novelty of freedom from restraint, and the desire for change (with which the most of us are affected), together with the charm of seeing and being seen, and having a good time generally, leads him to resort to devices of all kinds in order to gain favour with the powers that be, and to be selected as the next lucky man to be placed on the road. It is told of a young man in England, who was the senior of his department, who had repeatedly solicited the "guvener" for the position, that the "guvener" becoming tired of his constant solicitations, thought to wind him up by promising that when he became a sufficiently good salesman to sell white for black, he would put him on the road.

An opportunity soon presented itself to our senior, when a fashionable lady called and wished to be shown some mourning goods. Our obliging shopman stepped up and said, "Do you wish to be shown the very latest thing in mourning goods, ma'm?" On her replying that she did, he proceeded to show her some white goods. She says "You have mistaken me, sir. I wish to see mourning goods." "Yes, ma'm," he replied, "white is the very latest fashion for mourning goods." Our senior's assistants, looking, thought that he surely must have gone crazy, but he cooly told the lady that he would be very pleased to show her black goods, as they had plenty of them, that they would be glad to get rid of them, as they were not saleable now, but that if she wanted the newest thing for mourning, white was the correct thing. "Well," the lady said, "if it is the fashion, I will take it." It was cut off, paid for, and our delighted senior, with one of his assistants marched into the counting house, and announced to the "guvener" that he had succeeded in selling white for black, and had his assistant to witness it. He expected him to carry out his promise, which, to his credit be it said, he did, and our friend is now a successful "commercial" and an honour to our number.

Well, you will think we are a long time getting to Brantford. We are not there yet, nor will we be until I describe the commercial occupants of our car, and as I intend devoting a chapter to this subject, you can turn over the page.

### THE DIFFERENT KINDS.

In this car there were a variety of commercials, for there is as much variety in the travellers themselves as the businesses they represent. We may classify the travellers as belonging to one of the following "kinds of commercials:"

The Heavy Commercial.
The Polite Commercial.
The Noble Commercial.
The Green Commercial.
The Eccentric Commercial.
The Nervous Commercial.
The Lazy Commercial.
The Antiquated Commercial.
The Persevering Commercial.
The Spreeing Commercial.
The Religious Commercial.
The Industrious Successful Commercial.

I cannot say we had a representation of each class as above in the car with us, but there were two or three that would fill the bill. Our friend L——, who sat a few seats in front of us must be acknowledged as one of our

### "HEAVIES."

Of such there are only a few, so they are easily recognized. The "Heavy" wears the latest cut garments, the newest thing in hats, usually sports kid gloves, and sometimes an eye-glass, "you know," puts up at all the first-class hotels, smokes the finest flavored Havanas—no early Yorks or drumheads for him—attracts a good deal of attention, giving his orders to "Bob," the porter, in the "heavy" manner, only doing business with the leading and heaviest dealers in the place, and only visiting the leading and more important towns.

We approach him. "How do you do, L.?" "Ah B., how do do, old fellah? Glad to see you, 'you know.' Can't beah this howid twavelling, a fellah has to put up with so much, 'you know.'"

We advise him to give it up, as we always thought him to be more ornamental than useful. And it will generally be found that these *great men* abroad are but small men at home. They "patronize" the firm they are so gracious as to travel for, and finally leave the world as poor as when they entered it. This is usually the end of the "Heavy."

### THE POLITE COMMERCIAL.

Such a one as our friend C. We admire politeness and polite people. But some commercial travellers rather overdo the thing in their anxiety to create a favorable impression with "big guns" of merchants, who, in our opinion, are as much honoured by being called upon by us as we are to be received kindly and politely by them. We give a fair sample of the polite commercial in the following:

"Ah, good morning, Mr. White. Very glad indeed to see you, sir. Hope yourself, Mrs. White and family, are well. Ah, yes, glad to see you are quite busy; will do myself the honour of calling again." (Bows and scrapes, and backs out politely.)

Too subservient by half. It would look better for commercials to display more politeness and attention to each other and the general public than put it on too thick (too thin, we think) to court favor with buyers. Such men's actions are easily seen through. The gauze is transparent. This butterfly business won't wear. Come out in your true colors, and be a man among men. Retain the true ring of genuine politeness and manhood, and you will command the respect and friendship of all right-thinking men, and you will not break your back by stooping so low, when God intended you to walk upright. Be a man.

## THE NOBLE COMMERCIAL.

I am proud to say that our number comprises some of the above class—men with hearts big with love and kindness; men who would grace any walk in life; men of intellect, who never forget that they are gentlemen, and always act the part of one; men whom you would be proud to meet and be enabled to call friend; men who can command the "entrée" of our best drawing-rooms, and converse with intelligence on any subject touched upon, who can handle all knotty points in a masterly style, who have seen life in its broadest sense, and are conversant with every topic—moral, social, political or commercial. These are men who have proved themselves noble by nature, if not by birth. And as we will have to show a few of the shortcomings of our boys, we deem it right that our many perfections should be mentioned. It is told of a certain "commercial"—we will call him Jones—that he had not been an economical man on "the road," and had, like the majority of us, saved very little, and that meeting a brother commercial, one of the right sort, at one of our hotels, in the course of conversation he told this friend that through his good nature he had become security for a relation for five hundred dollars. Remorseless creditors would not wait, and when Jones left home the bailiff was about to descend on his home. Indeed, despair possessed himself and wife, and utter ruin stared them in the face. Still, the bailiff might wait a little and Jones might borrow the money elsewhere. But while they were at dinner that day, and while counting over a roll of money given him by a customer for the house, a telegram was brought to him. Our friend watched him read it. He turned pale, and a feeling of blank despair seized him. Seeing that something was very wrong, our friend said: "What is it Jones, my boy? Come, old fellow, don't give way—come, cheer up." "Read that," he said, with a husky, choked utterance, as he handed the telegram. It read as follows:—" The bailiff is in the house. Find the five hundred dollars by some means, or we must be turned into the street in a few hours." Handing him back the telegram, our friend looked at the haggard man as he nervously clutched the money belonging to his employer. He murmured: "I could return it in a few days some how—." Then there was a struggle between vice and virtue, and it was a terrible combat, but virtue won. As a bright smile came on his countenance he said, " Wife, I will not disgrace you. Jones, I will not stain the character you have upheld for twenty years. Welcome ruin rather than this." " Bravo, Jones ; you are of the right kind, and on the strength of your honesty, come with me, and arrangements shall be made to free you from your liabilities.' This was done, and in the course of time, Jones paid our friend every cent of the debt. Do you not call him a noble commercial? Great was his temptation to do wrong, but greater was his victory. The reader will remember the terrible railway accident that happened near Cornwall a few years ago: when the train, going at a great rate of speed, jumped the track, and the engine, mail and second-class cars were piled up in one mass of *debris*, when the scalding steam escaping from the engine, carried pain and death to the occupants of the cars. During the whole of that terrible night, with the *debris* piled up for bonfires, Mr. S., of Montreal, a commercial tra-traveller, worked like a hero—running from one wounded and agonizing scene to another, assisting one here and carrying another there—even stripping himself of his own shirt for bandages. This was self-denying enough. But S. himself was badly wounded, yet went at his glorious work full of love and self-denial. When at last morning relieved him, he was forced to leave the scene of

## DIFFERENT KINDS OF COMMERCIAL TRAVELLERS. 19

agony and horror, and he fainted from loss of blood, and it was months before S—— again took the road. His firm, however, (more success to them) paid him his salary all the time he was laid up. Do you not call these noble deeds?

It is told of another commercial while on a trip to a seaboard town, he was attracted by a crowd, in the midst of which there was a drunken old woman, and around her a lot of ruffians whose occupation for the time being seemed to be to tease the poor creature. By and by, teasing became too tame for the lambs, and one tall black scoundrel began to ill-treat her, whereupon she set up a genuine howl of pain. All at once the commercial leaped into the ring, and to the astonished crowd said: "Shame on you! shame on you! Do you call yourselves men? Why, you are worse than a horde of savages. Where is the police?" "Bonnet the fellow—give him one on his bread basket, Charley! hit him on the mug!" "Stand off you blackguards, have you no mothers of your own?" "I have be jabers," said an Irish sailor, as he followed our friend's example and leaped into the ring. "They'll have two mugs to punch now." But this man of the sea added prudence to valour and piped a stirring imitation of a boatswain's whistle, the police were soon on the spot, and the old woman near dead with fright, welcomed the police with thankfulness.

This gentleman was one of the most rolicking men of "the road," but possessed of the true spark of nobility. Besides Noble Commercials, we have, in plenty, men whose face and actions pronounce them all that is admirable in manhood, men who would scorn an ignoble action, who would not sully their honour though they are engaged in trade. For such men as these **we are** grateful, and if they do sometimes **put on a** little more style than is needful, we will pardon this in consideration of the highmindedness, and the true spirit of gentility which they bring into our midst. We **have** elevated the calling of a Commercial Traveller into one of the **most** honourable employments in the trading world, and we now find it more of a profession than a trade. When such men as **Lord** Dufferin classes himself with us, remarking that he was out here representing the house of Guelph & Co., pushing their interests, visiting their clients in the different sections, &c., **we may** well feel that we have in our number Noble Commercials.

### THE GREEN COMMERCIAL.

Some houses have been green enough to send upon the road to represent them green commercials, or rather youths whose business experience must be limited, if we add that nature sometimes has **not** been lavish of her mental gifts, supplying the raw material of the green commercial. You **can** easily pick him out, he is restless, uneasy, and does **not** seem to feel at home, he is not *au fait* in many things indispensable to free and easy travelling.

**This class is** small in number. **As a rule,** the firm pick the cutest youth they can lay their hands on, if they are up to snuff themselves, but occasionally manifest bad judgment, as all are liable to err. But though he may be green, he may learn rapidly, if his senses are on the alert, and perhaps learn more than is good for him.

The green commercial is known by his hesitation to enter a shop, and by his nervous bashfulness while there. The nervous sensation at first is a strong one. Being new they know every eye is upon them, criticising their appearance, comparing them in their minds with their predecessors, and forming conclusions before they know them. When a new traveller takes the ground previously canvassed by a good representative, he invariably appears at a disadvantage, because, whatever his personal qualifications may be, he *is not* his predecessor, who the boys all know well, and is therefore not in the same favor for the time being. He has not learned anything that entitles him to favor, nor done anything which could cause him to be received with open arms. In fact, he must win his reputation, work to make friends, and toil for success, before he can command it. Let him console himself, it will be the same for his successor.

Be of good cheer, green friend, the time will come when you will walk into every store with perfect freedom and with courteous politeness and dignity. Confidence in yourself is the first requisite to success. Think well of yourself, or perhaps no one else will. There are a host of commercials, and you must make your mark if you hope to succeed at all. The sooner you shed your green, grub-like covering, the sooner you will emerge a full-fledged commercial. If you have not the age you must appear to have. Walk into the hotel office, sign your name, hang up your hat with boldness, enter the dining-room, and draw up your chair to the table with such decision that old ones will say, "Well, he's not a green un,' anyway."

### THE ECCENTRIC COMMERCIAL.

There are travellers whom we would judge by their eccentric actions to have missed their profession. There is a well known Irishman, Mr. D., who, upon one of his journeys, found a certain hotel full, and was forced to occupy a double-bedded room with Mr. H., of Simcoe. This he decidedly objected to, and his mind was busy concocting a scheme by which he could have the room to himself, and teach the hotel people not to put any one in the same bedroom with him again. So he said to the clerk: "Mr. H. had better not sleep with me. I am very much given to doing strange things in the night, making rows, queer noises, and uttering strange cries." "Well, sir, Mr. H. must sleep in your room, nevertheless." Mr. H. did so, and was allowed to have one hour's clear rest before he retired. Our hero let midnight pass, and then when he heard that H. was lightly sleeping, he rose up in bed and muttered, like a maniac, with a husky voice and closed teeth: "Ha! ha! what's the use of living? No money, no orders, nothing. Let me die! What is life! Bah! it is a farce. What is it worth? Not a rap. Let me have done with it. Ha! ha! what is that blue glass that I see by the moon's rays. A razor! a razor! Let me clutch it. There's a passport from earth to hell. There are no travellers there—no employers there—no customers there." He arose from his bed, and the affrighted H. almost ceased to breathe, and his hair stood on end like

"Quills on the fretful porcupine."

Watching his every movement, D. went to the dresser, took up the razor, forcibly pressed it over the strop, and muttered with low and fearful distinctness: "I know what I'll do, cut that poor beggar's throat, that fool in the bed, and then cut my own. Bah! of what consequence is that miserable wretch's existence to him. The world can do without him." Apparently that "miserable wretch" was of quite another opinion, and proved it by stealing out of bed and gliding to the door, opened it, and bolted along the hall with the speed of the wind. D. dropped the razor, and all intentions of severing his windpipe, and his connection with things earthly. Quietly locking the door, retired to bed with the firm belief that his Simcoe friend would not trouble him any more that night. Meanwhile H. sped to the landlord's room and made known to the half sleeping host that Mr. D. was a madman—"going to cut his throat—my throat and his own—frightened for my life—had to run—cut his throat by this time—oh, lord!" said H., as his teeth chattered, and his knees knocked together. The landlord, knowing D., suspected how it was, but humouring H., returned to the double-bedded room, yet profound silence reigned within. "There, I told you," said H., "no doubt he's done it now—not a sound to be heard. Ugh, I think I see that gleaming razor even this very moment." " Well, it's no use bothering now if he's done it, we must wait until morning, and then send for the police," said the host. H. had to locate himself on the sofa the remainder of that sensational night. D. slept the sleep of the just and ingenious. In the morning the landlord insisted that D. must have committed suicide, but he saw through the joke when D. said, "in future please give me a room to myself." It is related of another eccentric commercial, that he had the honour of representing a firm that manufactured beer, and that going out on a certain journey, his employers say, " Belden you are going to ——. This journey you must get that money from old Anderson ; he has had too much credit already. You know we *must* get it!" " All right then, I won't come away without it." Belden in due course reached ——, and as he drove up put up at Anderson's for two days. At the end of the second day Belden disturbed the innkeeper in his devotion to the shrine of Sir Walter Raleigh. Boniface was puffing away philosophically when Belden advanced, bill in hand. " Guvener says, we must have this money, Mr. Anderson." " *Must* have it, eh! Tell him he can't get it at present." " But I am determined to have it." " Then if you mean to get it you may *whistle for it.*" Belden no sooner heard the instruction than he proceeded to put it into practice. He was a very good whistler it so happened, and mounting a block of stone outside the hotel, stuck his hands in his pockets and commenced whistling a series of airs, Nancy Lee, Pinafore, &c., which attracted around him a crowd of admiring listeners. Speculation was rife as to who the well-dressed mendicant who worked hard for his living could be, and many pitied him. "Beg pardon, sur, I be a poor man sur, but I be mighty sorry to see you come down like this 'ere, and if so be sur as you'll accept these two or three coppers, you're kindly welcome for sure!" "My friend, are you married," said Belden, stopping his performance for a minute. "Ese, sur, I've got a good wife un foine little uns, sur." Then keep your coppers, keep your coppers, my friend, you'll need them all." " Well, sur, no offence I hope, sur. I ax yer parding sur." " All right my friend, no offence," said B., " only don't interrupt my concert any more," as he resumed his musical rehearsal. The crowd swelled to enormous numbers, interrupting the regular traffic. Presently one of the magistrates of the town approached the scene and viewed this interference with vehicular progress frowningly. The magistrate, addressing one of the crowd, said, "Good people what is all this row about; what does it mean?" "I can't say for sure, sur. He woant accept no coppers, sur."

"Excuse me, sir, one moment please, why do you go on in this irregular way?" "Do you particularly want to know?" "I do, and moreover I *must* know. I am a magistrate and cannot allow you to block the road up by collecting such a crowd." "Well, sir, the man inside there owes me fifty dollars for beer," he says, " If I want the money for it I may *whistle for it*. By George, I shall go on doing so for the next twenty years unless he forks it over."

"Make way good people until I see the refractory debtor." Forcing his way to where Anderson was, he stated the case, narrating what was going on outside, and then said : " The fellow is spoiling your credit, you see, and advertising the fact that you won't pay him to all the town, and if you don't pay him he'll go on whistling to the crack of doom to all appearances, the man seems to be made of bellows and pipes—it won't do you know. The astonished Boniface at once went for his keys, and soon got the money. After receiving which B. descended from his pedestal. Next morning as the beer traveller was driving off, Anderson said, " I say Beldon, you have not paid me my bill yet. I want my money." Belden replied, " you may do as you told me to do for mine, *whistle for it*."

### THE NERVOUS COMMERCIAL.

Spare me from journeying with this gentleman. He will give you a lovely time of it, everthing goes wrong, everybody to blame. You may know him by his restless eye and uneasy ways. He commences his fits of nervousness as soon as he appears on the turf. Breakfast not being ready to the moment, he paces around like a caged lion, he feels afraid he will be too late for his first customer, although he has plenty of time. He is continually fretting lest he will be too-late. He cannot take things coolly, he fears that every conveyance will leave before he gets on it. He is always afraid that the up train will run into the down train, and a short sharp whistle from the engine will cause him to jerk the window up and out goes his head. He is unfit for the road, and ought to stop at home and grace a circle of admiring friends who could anticipate his wishes; his fidgity, unquiet disposition constantly brings discomfort to all around him. We are therefore constrained to believe that this particular class would be far better gracing some other walk in life. Take our advice friend, retire.

### THE LAZY COMMERCIAL.

There are a few of this class, but they do not as a rule last long on the road, their services "don't pay." On arriving at the hotel they are the first to greet you, as they are always to be found sitting around. They are the last to turn out of bed in the morning, and a late breakfast is in order, after which the morning paper must be read, and then a saunter up town to call upon a customer, who he finds has gone down to the hotel to see his opposition friend's samples, and if afterwards he does succeed in seeing him he finds that he has ordered all he wants in his line. Had he seen him earlier he might have got the order. He is promised orders for the next trip, which he usually never gets. He is always behind getting his samples packed, consequently late at the ticket office, giving others a good deal of trouble. He is usually a good natured soul, he will listen to all your grievances, and sympathize with you. His advice and experience are at your disposal, but in a few trips we miss him, he has gone where lazy people are more useful. It is with him as it was with a new Scotch traveller not long out, got a sit. and was sent west to push trade in sections where his countrymen predominated, county of Bruce for instance. He returned to give an account of his stewardship. "How do you like travelling, Sandy?" said a young sprout in the warehouse, after he had been out five weeks and returned minus orders. "Oh!" says Sandy, "I likit the travelling gay weel, ye ken. The vittals was guid, and the companie was weel eneuch, the change was pleasant, the dinners fine, man, and the 'whiskey' was no that bad whatever, but when yo came to seekin' orders man it was *awfu' like beggin'*."

### THE ANTIQUATED COMMERCIAL.

We have not many of this type in this country, as the institution is comparatively young here—although we met a traveller the other day in Chatham who told us he was celebrating his twenty-fifth anniversary. He formerly had his own team, and would leave Montreal for a six months' pilgrimage, (we hope for his wife's sake that he was not a married man then), and drive through to Windsor—doing business all the way through. He still sticks to it, and is likely to continue to the end of the chapter. We have reference in this connection to the old school of travellers, whom you will recognize in the eminently respectable looking gentleman of sixty or thereabouts. His hair is as white as snow, and betokens years of experience; his nose is—well, we will say *red*, and we wonder whether it would fiz if it were to come into contact with cold water. The Antiquated will tell you that "Commercial Travellers are not what they were, sir; (snuffs) not what they were, sir. They send out any sort of fledgling now, sir, and have as much impudence, sir, as would have served half a dozen in my time, sir." He can tell you of all the notables of the road who lived in his time. He doesn't know much of our modern celebrities. The Antiquated is in his element if he chance to meet another Antiquated. They will entertain each other and mutually console each other with tales of the good old days when they were boys together. "Things are not as they used to be forty years ago," when he first travelled. According to him, the machinery of existence is out of order, and he simply tolerates the present—evidently considering himself a representative of the "glorious past." But we have exceptions, even in the Antiquated. Every Commercial must have met him in the person of our esteemed friend, John Barr, a genial, jolly old fellow—one of the "good old kind," who laughs at discomfort, and when with the younger fraternity, feels himself a juvenile once more; who sympathizes with their ideas, pardons their weaknesses, joins heartily in the conversation, and when with them forgets his age. Such a jolly "old brick," he is, as the boys say, that we instinctively accord to him precedence and respect on every occasion. He deserves all posts of honour, he talks affectionately to the boys, and his customers ; they like to see the good-natured, genial old fellow ; he manages to extract good out of everything, and we respect him for his kindly disposition and for his age.

## THE PERSEVERING COMMERCIAL.

"Men are accused of not knowing their own weakness, yet perhaps as few know their own strength. Sometimes there is a vein of gold which perseverance unearths." We presume it is quite unnecessary to say that the very first requisite for a successful traveller is *perseverance*, or, in short, *push*. In spite of this recognized requisite, many young men are sent out who have not mastered the first letter in the alphabet of commercial enterprise. Like undrilled recruits sent out to join the ranks of a well-drilled army, they are out of place, and are no benefit to their employers or themselves. I well remember my first trip on the road—how anxiously looked forward to for a week or so previous. Going on a strange errand, bound to strange places, having to associate with gentlemen unknown, and wanting the sometimes necessary form of introduction to all. For several days before the start, how nervous, agitated and anxious. New faces, new places, new scenes, flitted through my imagination. All was new to me, even the packing and unpacking, and the handling of my samples. At last the morning arrived I was to make a start. Passing a sleepless night, hearing the old St. Lawrence bell strike every hour, I was pleased when daylight came. After breakfast, of which I ate little, train time found me at the station in good tim

Here I found a chum or two to see me off. I confess I felt of a little importance. All was bustle and confusion (I take things cooler now); the station bell rings, I am aboard, the train moves, I am off on my "first journey." I get off at Weston, where I go through the form of having baggage up town and getting a sample room. I unpacked and arranged the samples on tables, when I had a little rehearsal to myself, trying to feel at home among the samples, and introducing them to the supposed buyer, talking them up, and booking a good order, " in my mind." *Push and pull* was the order of the day. On calling upon merchants, if I could not persuade them to accompany me to the hotel to see my samples, I would take the liberty of taking some of my leading lines into their store that they might see them; and I would work up so much enthusiasm into the introduction of my goods, that sometimes I thought that I imbued the merchant with the same feeling, and made up their minds that the goods must be of value, so strong did I talk it. Others, I have thought, gave me a little order to reward my pluck and perseverance, so anxious did I seem to make my mark. I had made up my mind to be a success, as I felt my future depended upon it. Some, perhaps, gave me a little order to get rid of me. I remember, in my first journey, visiting Elora, and calling upon the firm of ―――― & Clark. As usual, I asked for the buyer, who I found to be Mr. Clark (who is now, by the way, speaker of the local legistature) The young gentleman told me Mr. Clark was at his house, laid up with a sprained ankle. I asked if I could see him if I went up to his house. He thought I could; so I went up to Mr. Clark's house, and was ushered into his parlor, where I found him lying on the sofa. I announced my business, saying I represented a young and enterprising firm who were very anxious to do business with him, and that I would bring up some of my best lines of samples, and show them to him, if he would take the trouble to look at them. To this he kindly agreed, and I brought him, with the help of the hotel porter, two bags full of samples, which I spread out on the floor of his parlor, and from which he selected a number of lines, giving me a nice little order, which was the commencement of a business with the firm, which was continued afterwards, to their mutual advantage I hope, and which sent me on my way rejoicing, and proved a reward for perseverance.

A friend of ours, the now justly celebrated T. F. Kingsmill, now the largest and most successful dry-goods merchant in London, one time represented the leading wholesale dry-goods house of Hamilton, and, in course of his travels, called upon M., of Berlin. On presenting his card to M. the latter quietly looked at it, and then as quietly tore it up and threw it into K's. face. "Thanks," said K., "the house expects me to sell you a good bill." "Well, you'll not sell me a cent, and there's the door." K. says, "I don't think I'll go out just yet," and he quietly seated himself on the counter. M. says, "I thought I told you to leave my store." K. says, "This is a place of business, and I don't purpose to leave until I get ready." M. says, "If you don't leave I'll put you out." K. says, "You have not got men enough in your employ, with you assisting them, to put me out." (K. was about right, as he weighs twenty ounces to the pound, and good, honest, solid English beef at that. K. sees a plug of tobacco on the shelf behind him, reaches over and takes it, and, taking a large carving-knife, commences cutting the tobacco and filling his pipe; while M. marched up and down the floor like a caged lion. By the time K. had finished his smoke, M. had cooled down considerably, when K. said: "You might as well go and see my samples first as last, as I will not leave the store until you do." Said M., "It seems that I have got to do what you tell me, so come on," and in the end K. sold him a nice bill, and they drank each other's health, and parted good friends. So much for perseverance.

The same gentleman, our friend Kingsmill, arriving in town one evening, and while partaking of tea overheard two other commercials conversing about what they were doing and what they intended doing. One had been sent up by a firm to sell a merchant of the town a bill of goods, as he had written down to say that he would be glad to see the traveller if in that section, as he was out of many lines of goods, and was unable to leave home to visit the market. Our two young friends proposed to pass the evening with a game of billiards, while our old cove slipped out and got his samples brought up from the station and taken to the said merchant's store, whither he repaired, and knowing he wanted goods, from what he had overheard, had the underhold, said: "My dear Mr. W., it is very important that I should reach P. to-morrow by the early train leaving here. I will make it worth your while to look at my samples to-night." W. agreed, and K. booked the order intended for our young gent. who was passing his evening playing billiards. K. left in the morning, by the first train, and when our young friend found time to call on W. in the morning, he found to his surprise and disgust, that he had ordered all he wanted the previous evening. Be up and doing, young man, next time, and get the reward of perseverance.

It is told of a certain traveller, in the hardware line, visiting Paisley, calling upon a merchant named P., introducing himself and the house he represented, about as follows :—

"Mr. P., I believe."

P. condescends to nod.

"I am representing W. McG. & Co., of Hamilton, in hardware. Mr. McG. has done a great deal for this section of the country in helping to build the W. G. and B. railway."

P.—" What has that to do with me?"

"Oh nothing, I suppose, but he thought the merchants in this section would appreciate what he had done, and patronize him accordingly."

P.—" Well, I don't want any of his hardware"

"I would like very much to show you our samples, sir."

P.—" I don't want to see your samples or you either, and you better get out."

"Certainly, sir, if you desire me."

P.—"Well, I do, and the sooner the better."

Well this kind of reception was enough to dampen the ardour of any ordinary traveller. Not so our friend of the hardware. For next trip, when in Paisley, he goes in to see P. again. "Good day Mr. P., I represent Mc G. & Co., of Hamilton. The last time I was here you gave me an order, and I hope you were satisfied with the way it was filled?"

"W. McG. & Co., of Hamilton. W. McG. & Co., of Hamilton. I don't remember of having bought anything from that firm."

"No," said the traveller, "but you gave me an order which I think I filled to your satisfaction. You ordered me out, and I went out." This brought a smile to P's face.

"Well," says he, "I'll give you an order this time."

And then and there bought a nice little bill of goods from him. So much for perseverance.

I was in the fancy goods line, and had called several times upon R. of B., but with always the same result. C. began to think that R. was willingly shutting his eyes to numerous advantages, and was injuring himself thereby. C. stuck to him one trip most valiantly, and again and again tried to get R. to look at his samples. R. at last got riled, says, "I tell you for the last time, I want nothing at all."

"But, sir, surely you'll look at my samples some time?"

"No I won't. I don't want any of your goods. Can't you take a courteous refusal?"

"Yes, sir, certainly, but you would confer a great favour on me personally if you would have the kindness to even look at my samples. I've got a splendid lot of——"

Then a lady customer came in, and R. went off to attend to her, leaving C. very abruptly, and sang out very insolently:

"Come and show them to me then at three o'clock in the morning."

"Thank you, sir, very much obliged, good morning."

"Thank goodness," says R. "I have got rid of that pest. He is the most **persevering** dog I ever met." C. said nothing, but retired very early that night, after having arranged with the night watch to call him promptly at 2.30. In a few minutes he was dressed and had a case of samples on a truck, landed at R's. door at three o'clock precisely, just as the town clock was striking. C. commenced to kick vigorously at R's. door. A policeman came along and wanted to know why C. was acting in this manner. C. assured him he was acting up to orders. Mr. R. had asked him to come there at three o'clock to show him some samples. C. commenced kicking again, and kept up the bombardment until a window was raised up stairs, (as R. lived over the store) and a head was thrust out of the window.

"What the devil are you kicking up that row about."

"Beg pardon, sir, are you not Mr. R."

"Yes. I am—what do you want banging at my door like that?"

"I am here according to your orders, sir. It's just three o'clock now."

"Who the devil are you?"

"C.—Sir, here's all my samples waiting for you to look at them."

"I want nothing to do with you."

"Then if you don't fulfil your promise I shan't stop kicking."

"Come again during the day then, you persevering scoundrel."

"Do you promise me an order, on your word and honour then?"

"Yes, yes, said the infuriated R., slamming down the window.

C. goes back to the hotel and enjoys the balance of the night in sweet sleep, thinking of the promised order in the morning, which in calling for, Mr. R. gave him, as he was a gentleman of his word. He never repented of it, as the house was a good one, and C. a good fellow, and ever afterwards they have been doing business, and are now the best of friends. Again perseverance wins.

It is told of a sharp young fellow in the needle trade, who waited upon a certain merchant, whose shop had a door in the rear as well as in the front. The following conversation ensued:—"Good-morning, sir. I have the honour of representing so-and-so in the needle trade. I would like to show you my samples, **and do a** little business with you." "I want nothing in **your** line." "Perhaps **you** are not aware, sir, that I represent the greatest needle people in the world?" "Yes, I am quite aware of that, but I do not require any, and if I did, I am served very well where **I am buying** at present." "But, perhaps, you will be **good** enough to look at my samples, sir?" "I tell you I do not want any, and you annoy me **with** your persistence." "But if you would just favour me with a look, I think an order might—" "I'll give you an order, now leave my shop." "Certainly, sir," and bidding the gent good-morning, he made a speedy exit by the back door, but only to return **and** re-enter the shop by the front door—addressing the merchant as though he had never seen him before. "Good-morning, sir. I have the honour of representing Allcock, Laight & Co., in the needle trade. I hope to be able **to** do a little **business** with you." Confound you, sir, you were here only **this** very minute." "Yes sir, and then I had the pleasure of taking a very small order from you, which I hope was duly executed to your entire satisfaction. Any favour of a more business-like character and profitable nature shall have equally prompt attention." The customer burst into a laugh, and C. had turned the tables in his favor. The merchant cleared a space on his counter, and said :— "Well, you're about the most cheeky and original traveller I ever **met** with. But **come,** to reward you for your pertinacity, I'll give you **a** little order." Out came the needles **and order** book, and **a** small order was booked which led to larger ones, the seller and buyer parting equally pleased with each other. Even now they often relate the manner of the first sale and purchase. This young man was an "original," and, depend upon it, this class of men who understand human nature, make the most successful commercials. We have no desire to reflect on any nationality, as there are good travellers belonging to each, but Scotchmen are so uniformly persevering that their pertinacity is acknowledged.

It is said that a young Scotchman applying for a situation in New York, and betraying the least sign of his nationality in appearance or language, the keen, penetrating look of our thin-faced and experienced American cousin takes in the situation, and he says: "Young man, I have no desire for some time yet to part with my business. Go west, young man, go west."

An excellent example of perseverance is told of a Scotch traveller, hailing from Leith, and representing a Scotch tweed house.

On a very cold December day, Sandy interviewed a prospective customer, and pressed him very hard to look at his "wee bit cloth paittrens." After exhausting all his more subtle arguments, Sandy said: "Mon! you micht jist luik at ma paittrens; it wadna tak ye a minit."

"What's the good of wasting your time and mine? I want nothing."

"Ot, that disna mait'er, mon! If ye jist see ane, I ken ye'll buy a piece or twa."

"It's no use, I tell you! I wish you would take a denial, and not keep on bothering."

"Me maisther said to me, when he sent me oot, says he, 'Sandy, when ye get a likely customer, my lad, aye stick til him.' Noo, I think you're a likely chap to buy, and I maun jist dea as I'm tel't, ye ken."

"Don't you see my shop is full of customers, and you keep on bothering me like this."

"Well, ye canna serve customers richt unless ye hae the richt stuff, ye ken. Sae the sunner ye luik at ma paittrens, the better for ye baith."

"Will you go out of my shop, once for all?"

"No, me. I've come a' the way frae Leith to sell ye stuff, an' I'm no gaun awa' without trying what I can dea. Gang awa' man, an' serve yer costimers, I can wait —I'm in na hurry. Ye'll buy a piece—maybe twa."

"Be off with you, or I shall have to kick you out."

"Hech, sir, ye wadna do that. 'Twad be actionable, ye ken!"

"I'll do it for you, nevertheless, if you're not off, soon."

"Ma guidness! ye wadna dea't. Gang on the noo. I'll bide yer time, mon."

"Are you going, or are you not?"

"No' jist at present, ma maunie. I maun show ye ma paittrens."

"Go, follow your cap, then," said the enraged shop-keeper, as he seized hold of Sandy's Glengarry and pitched it into the street, which was slush and mud.

Sandy uttered not a word. He simply left his bundle on the counter, and stroking down his hair, deliberately walked out into the street, picked up his cap, and as he came back into the shop with an unruffled countenance, brushing his unfortunate head covering, said to the merchant:

"Weel, as you've pitched oot ma cap intil the street, maybe ye'll be good eneuch to luck at ma samples the noo."

The people waiting to be served, and the merchant himself, even—all burst out into a hearty, good-natured laugh, at this instance of unruffled placidity under insult.

Sandy made pride subservient to interest, and never dreamed of allowing his muddy cap, nor his wounded feelings to stand in the way of selling a "bit or twa of tweed, ye ken." The popular feeling was all in Sandy's favor, and the merchant's customers strongly insisted that there must be something worth looking at in the bundle of the persevering Scotch traveller. So the merchant relented, and when the place was cleared, examined Sandy's samples of tweeds, and found them real good and cheap.

As a matter of course, virtue should always be rewarded, according to orthodox popular narration. Sandy booked an order. He now often relates this anecdote, and is proprietor of one of the finest estates in Scotland. He can afford to look back with equanamity on the days when he was struggling hard as a commercial. But he never forgets the Sandy of former days, since the same muddy cap hangs in a conspicuous place in his library. When any of his friends ask him why he takes so much care of that *old thing,* he replies that it is always to him an **emblem of** "Perseverance." For the experience in which that Glengarry played so conspicuous a part so impressed itself upon Sandy's mind that **he never** rested until he drove his nail home, and placed himself in **his** present high position. "**Go** thou and do likewise."

### THE SPREEING COMMERCIAL.

Alas! this class comprises a **few** of our number, and it is not to be wondered at, as they have to drink against the whole country—not only the merchants that are **so inclined, but** their clerks, and a host of acquaintances made on the road, each journey adding to the number, besides other commercial travellers. There is, perhaps, no calling where the opportunity **is** greater and the inducements more to treat **and** drink, meeting other travellers and friends always in hotels where it **is** to be had. The genial host, always glad to **see** you—"Won't you indulge?" The customer, after making a purchase, knows it **is** the custom **among** the craft to ask him to have a drink, and **thus it** goes on, from morning until evening, and sometimes does not end with evening, for a few of the boys get together and keep it up till morning. In this class are the brightest fellows we have among us—**good** fellows, a few have "weathered the storm" for a **good** while, but it is leaving its mark on them. It is only a question of time with most of them. Like the lazy commercial, they do not last long—cannot make it pay, and thus eventually must make room for others who, though not so bright **and** clever, send in more orders, which is the "one thing needful." A volume could be written about them—the scrapes they get into, and those they get out of. Windsor seems to be a weak point for "the boys." Arriving there, they seem to lose their balance; whether it is because they are so near the land of the free, and their spirits get elated with visions of Vanderbilt, Jay Gould & Co., or the perfumes of Walker's distillery, I do not know, but certain it is that houses "lose sight" of their men sometimes when in this locality. It is related of a certain house whose traveller lost his balance in Windsor, that another was sent up to take his samples and continue his journey, but, on meeting the old friend, a feeling of sympathy induced the new man to forget himself, and he likewise got on "the tare." As a last resort, a member of the firm went up to look after the "lost sheep," and it was not very long until he joined the happy pair, making a trio of "jolly good fellows," and they all had to have their spree out before any more ready-mades were sold. Another friend of the writer's, a brother of the proprietor of a wholesale dry goods house in Montreal, was representing the house in the west, reached Windsor, and for a time was lost to the firm. Some one was sent to look after him; they found the samples, but no traveller, and had come to the conclusion that the Detroit River alone could unravel the mystery, when, lo! at the end of thirty days, our hero turned up, having, during that time, acquired the accomplishment of making cane-bottom chairs in the Detroit Workhouse. When "on the spree," commercials, like the rest of humanity, are "not themselves at all." Another friend of ours, a big fellow in the millinery line, meeting a number of farmers one evening in Dunnville, announced that he was a new wheat buyer, and that he was prepared to pay two or three cents a bushel more than the local men. It was Saturday afternoon, and he was going to commence operations on Monday morning. You know the farmer's weakness on the price of wheat; they won't drive a few miles farther for a cent or two a bushel—oh, no! Monday morning brought such a string of teams into Dunnville as had not been seen there at once for some time before. As the news of the new wheat buyer had circulated well on Sunday (I do not suppose that the old fellows said anything about it at church, but it got around), and the turn-out was creditable to them. They were all eager to show "*their samples*" to the new buyer, but he was not to be found. Millinery suited him better than wheat, and he was on the sell, instead of buying. It would not have been well for him, if some of his agricultural friends had got hold of him that morning.

A particular friend of ours, who was addicted to spreeing on the road, found himself, at the end of one, in rather an uncomfortable predicament. He was entrusted by the firm to proceed to New York on a purchasing tour (and let me here say, for the benefit of employers, all things being equal, there is no man so fit to buy goods as those who have to sell them). After packing his valise, and kissing his wife and little ones good bye, with a well-filled purse to pay his expenses, we find him on board the 3:45 train leaving Toronto, with a through ticket for New York. Arriving at Hamilton, without incident, he changes cars, and on entering the train he was delighted and surprised to find seated there an old friend and companion, who, for the last few years had resided in the land of the free. "Well, J. W., old boy, how are you, and whither bound?" "Going to New York to pick up some goods for the house." "Glad to hear it, as I am bound for New York too." "Good! and we will lay ourselves out to have a good time." "Say we commence it by going and getting a drink; and, by the way, I want to buy two or three bottles of good brandy while in Canada, as, you know, you have the 'correct thing' in brandies in Canada." Oh! had our friend remembered his weakness right here, and brought to mind the promises he made to his dear little wife that morning, when leaving home, how much misery he would have spared himself and friends! But, no; drown conscience, and please your so-called friend: "I'll take a little gin and sugar, please. What is yours to be?" "Oh, I'll sample the best brandy; and say, bartender, give me two bottles of Hennessey." "All aboard, going East" was heard, and our friends rush out and into their train. Pleasant conversation ensues, when the friend proposed to draw the corks of the brandy bottles, to avoid duty, and while the corks are out to have a taste. Of course, by frequent tasting, by the time they reach Buffalo they are up to any "little game," and it was proposed to remain there over night and "take in" the city. It is needless to recount their doings that night. Next day they were arm-in-arm, on a glorious spree, which they continued, finding their way to Boston and Saratoga, whither they went to have a little bathing, see the sights, and sober off.

Our friend came to his senses after a week's carousing, waking up one morning to find his watch and valuables gone, and not a cent in his pockets. The thought of his position, and its consequences with the firm at home, more than sobered him, and he devoted his morning to planning how he would get out of this scrape. As a last resort for funds, he made a thorough search in all his pockets, and to his unspeakable joy and surprise, found in one of his vest pockets the sum of one dollar and fifty cents. But what earthly use would this sum be to him? He did not want to write to the firm for money, as this would expose him; nor did he want to let his Mary know what he had been doing. He took a stroll to collect his ideas, and in passing through the streets he met a great number of the beauty and fashion on their "morning parade," all beautifully and richly dressed. It was a hot July day, and fans were in keeping with the day. He noticed an immense pile of palm leaf fans in passing a store. The idea struck him to buy his money's worth of these, and sell them at a profit to "raise the wind;" for who is so inventive and ingenious as the commercial in straitened circumstances. He turned the thing over in his mind as often as he turned the money over in his pocket, and at last concluded that he would make the venture. So, repairing to the store, he made the best

## THE SPREEING COMMERCIAL.

"dicker" he could for his money, getting them at fifty cents per dozen. He takes his bundle and starts for the beach, where the fashionable ladies were enjoying the sea air. He takes his stand, and as any ladies pass, offers them, in an exceedingly polite manner, "Palm leaf fans only fifty cents each." Some bright, sparkling, laughing creatures passing were attracted by the novelty of a person selling palm leaf fans at fifty cents each, and buy one "just for a lark."

Sold again, who will have another one, only a few dozen left. "I say, Gussey, come here, here is a *real gentleman* selling fans; such a lark," and rushing to another group of young ladies, and delights them with the news that a *real* gentleman is on the beach selling fans. "Let's all go and buy one, girls, just for the fun of the thing." Says Grace, "if he should turn out to be a real count doing this on a wager, I shouldn't wonder but that is the very thing, for you know these foreign counts are so eccentric and do such funny things, it must be so, girls, as no poor person would have the audacity to ask fifty cents for a palm leaf fan." The news spread to the hotel like wildfire. Ladies hastened to the beach and purchased a fan perhaps from a count (it counted to our friend), for the profit on every fan told on the amount of his pile. Who of the ladies could help buying a fan from him, he was so gentlemanly. "Here we are again. Who'll have the next one, only fifty cents each, the real original, only a few left. Sold again (Yes both the fan and the purchaser.)" By evening our friend sold out the line, netting him a profit of sixteen dollars and fifty cents, with which amount he made his way to New York, where he wrote the firm and his dear old girl, that since his arrival he had been sick, but was now better, and to do him justice he was sick of what he had done. However, he went to work, energetically transacted his business, and returned to Toronto, to receive the embraces of his loved ones and the congratulation of the firm on recovering his health and strength. He is now a bright and shining light among us, and we doubt if the house ever knew anything about it. But let us hope that the lesson taught him will be a warning against repeating his Saratoga experience.

Not long ago three commercials in H., after having engaged a good dinner, adjourned to the billiard-room in order to have a game while they were enjoying their after dinner smoke. "Let us play for the drinks," said J., "agreed." So they had the drinks while the game progressed, of course, the one who got "stuck" would have another, and of course, another drink, game after game, and drink after drink. "By Jove," says J., "I don't intend to do another stroke to day ; and as I've had a good journey thus far, I'm blowed if I do either," says L.," "and I'll throw up the sponge, too, for this afternoon," says S.

"Say we play for a dollar a game to make it interesting." All agreed ! So they played all afternoon, S. and L. both loosing a good round sum, and J. of course, so much the winner. Evening coming on, J. proposed to pay the tickets to the Mechanics' Hall, where a play was going on. Occupying a prominent seat, by a constant use of their opera glasses, and their loud comments on the play, drew upon them the eyes of the whole house, and attracted the attention of the usher, (for they were very ill-behaved and quite drunk), who came to them and told them if they were not better behaved they would have to leave the house. Of course, gentlemen could not be spoken to in that manner, and J., (who was on his muscle) hit Mr. Usher a rap on the eye, and commenced a row, which ended by the gents being ejected into the street. Once there a cab was called, and bundling in, cabby asked for instructions. " Drive ush to John street" shouted S. Cabby obeyed orders, and when there they being unable to get out, cabby asked, " where will I drive to now, gentlemen ?" " Drive ush't to King street."

That interesting locality arrived at, Cabby again said, in desperation, " Gentlemen, where do you wish to drive to ?" " Drive ush to th' Devil." Cabby, although he had heard of the locality, could not oblige them this time, and instead, drove them over to the police station, and interviewed the officer in charge : " Well, sir, what's your business, eh ?" " Plase, sir, thir is thra gints over fernint in moy cab." " And what have I to do with them ?" " Plase, sir, tha ingaged me to droive thim, and wan sais, 'Droive us to King strate;' and whin I get thair, another wan of them tells me to droive thim to John strate; and whin I gits thair, sis I, ' Where will I droive yes till now, gintlemen ?' So they says, ' Droive us to the Divil.' "

"Well, and what then?" "So, begora, I thought I'd bring 'em afore you, sir." "Indeed! Are they drunk?" "Indade, sir, it's moy opinion that they air." "Bring them in; we'll take care of them." The three were now so very drunk and helpless that it was a matter of carrying them in, and they spent the night in a police cell. Next morning, on awakening and coming to their senses, they were surprised at their surroundings. Instead of carpets, luxuries, and their little indispensables, they beheld the plainest and most uncomfortable necessaries, which had the effect of sobering them; and when, at the morning sitting of the Court, they were each fined a dollar and costs, they comprehended that they had been on a drunk. If this had been any lesson to them, it would have been cheap. But, no. "Jolly good lark," says J. "A sort of thing you read about, but seldom experience," says S. "Oh, let us be happy and gay, boys." This comes from L. Hardly any signs of repentance in these remarks, you will observe.

"Let's go and have a game of cards," says L. "Just the cheese," chimes in the others. Away they go to the hotel, and commence their little game, From playing loo they indulge in a little bluff, and the result was J. got broke, and gave L. his I-O-U for thirty dollars, and if S. was not broke, he was nearly so. After dinner, at which all knew their state, and what they had been up to, they hire a hack and drive to D., when they went in for a big time, singing, dancing, drinking, and a general jam-be-ree. Money spent freely, customers and business neglected, **and character going to the dogs as fast as possible.**

The conclusion of this notable spree is well known. J. left for the U. S., where, we since have learned, he was clerking in a dry goods store. **This spree ended his fashionable career.** His samples were taken possession of by a new man. S. and L. **carried on** their spree two or three **days** longer, when the following telegram was **received by the hotel**: "We have heard nothing from our **Mr. S.** these last few days. Do you know of his whereabouts?" To which they answered: "Not seen much of him since **Thursday.** His samples **are here;** but **at** present we do not know whether he is in town or not." Result: One of Mr. S's. firm arrives on the scene, finds out all that has transpired during the last **few** days, pays Mr. S's. bill, with a warning **as** to **any** future amount; stops the amount out of **the salary** due Mr. S, and, finally, when Mr. S. appears at the office of the firm, they settle **up, he** is discharged on the spot, and **given a** lecture which ought **to serve him for** the balance **of his natural life.** He drops out **of our ranks** and has **been lost sight of.** L. manages **to** get **his** traps together and struggle on as far **as B., where he** was taken **very ill, as** a natural consequence **of such a** spree. For three weeks he **lay in a** raging **fever. His** life was in danger. His wife came to him to cheer, soothe and comfort him, nurse him and forgive him, after he had opened his heart to her and confessed his wickedness. She proved his guardian angel and trusty friend, fighting the fever until, by God's mercy, she had the pleasure of seeing him on his way to recovery and health. His firm never knew the truth, but thought he had been spared through a long illness, and wrote to him, congratulating him on his recovery. The lesson was not lost on him, however, as he profited by his experience and afterwards became a teetotaler.

There is still another case I want to give—not so much to show up the weakness of our "boys," as to have them profit by the experience of others, and to let them see what is the result of "spreeing" among commercials. In my time on the road I can count by the dozens men of the finest mental qualities, men gifted with no ordinary talent, men who would have graced our parliamentary halls, and men who could have risen to have filled the place of our present wholesale merchants, but who, through this one failing, have *missed their chance*, and dropped into obscurity—some of them into their graves. And the one of which I am about to write is now a day laborer on the Pacific Railway. All in the commercial line will remember him—we will call him Ruckelston—who at one time occupied the proud position of manager for one of the largest and oldest dry goods firms in Toronto. The failure of the firm caused R. to look around for something else to do, and he at last decided to take to *the road*. After trying other lines, he settled down to the ready made clothing line, and the ground he had to cover was the north, taking in the trip up the lake by boat, from Collingwood, and the far-famed town with "spreeing **travellers**," Owen Sound. Owen Sound, in the good old **days** of stage coaching, especially in winter, when travellers would be storm-bound for a week at a time, seemed to be so isolated from the civilized portion of Canada, and so far out of sight of employers, and so difficult to get information to and from, that some travellers made it a point to *bottle up* their spree and be steady and true until **they** reached Owen Sound, when they would *uncork* all their good resolutions, kick completely over the traces, to go **on** what is improperly termed a "glorious spree." So customary was it for commercials to spree in those days in Owen Sound. that the writer, on visiting a **family in** good circumstances, and moving in good society there, were shocked to find out that I was a commercial traveller, telling **me** that they had refused introductions to commercials at their firemen's ball, owing to the reputation of being drunkards that our fraternity enjoyed.

But, I am delighted to say, using the language of the Hon. Edward Blake, that "circumstances have changed," and so have commercial travellers; and we are proud to say, more especially as to this particular weakness—as a spreeing commercial is a very exceptional person in these days of commercial travelling. Excuse the diversion, but the mention of this town led me away from the subject, as it did the traveller from the path of temperance. Hard on Owen Sound, but we cannot help it; it was a true bill.

To return to our friend R., he, in company with

three other travellers, had reached Collingwood on the way north, and all hired teams to drive to Owen Sound. It was a cold, stormy, March day, and the start was made in good style from Charley Cameron's, R. leading the way, having a splendid pair of horses and a handsome trap, upon which was mounted his big clothing cases, and upon the top of them Ruckelstone and his valise, into which, before leaving, he had put a good bottle of brandy, to have a little along the road to keep out the cold. R. drove very well for a few miles, but he patronized the contents of the valise pretty often, and began to sing "Rule Britannia," a *sure sign* to those who knew him that he was beginning to feel the "effects." In pulling out the bottle again, and waving it on high, to drink the health of the gentlemen in the teams following, he dropped the lines, and the spirited horses, feeling their freedom, started off upon the run, R. hanging on for dear life, but still waving the bottle on high.

Of course, all were alarmed for his safety, and starting our horses on the run to endeavor, if possible, to overtake the runaways. They were approaching a turn in the road, nearing some woods, and, as we were contemplating the result, the horses turned. Over goes the sleigh, and the last thing we saw of R. he was flying through the air, bottle still in hand, followed by his valise and sample cases, and the horses freed, plunge through the snow into the woods. On arriving at the scene, we found things pretty well mixed. Poor R., in his headlong career, was nearly buried in the snow; his cases

were broken open, and their contents—linen dusters, etc.
—scattered promiscuously round on top of him. We uncovered him and righted him up; he was a little stunned, but in all the struggle had not lost his grip on the bottle, which he waved triumphantly over his head, giving us another stanza of " Rule Britannia." One followed the horses into the woods, and found them lovingly entangled in the underbrush, nothing the worse of wear. We righted up his sleigh, picked up his things, and got him into shape to proceed, after having to use our jack-knives and string in repairing the harness, etc. We decided that he had led the van long enough, and must, for the balance of the journey, " bring up the rear."

In due time we arrived in Owen Sound, and after shaking ourselves up, getting thawed out, and partaking of a good hot supper at the Coulson House, with a lot of other good souls, R. of course related his adventure of the afternoon to an admiring group of fellow commercials that night, who decided to celebrate the event with three times three. Amongst the number, one or two convivial spirits, who, like a magazine, only wanted a match to touch them off, met their match in R., who opened the ball with a bottle of wine, which was followed in due course by another and another. The next morning the irrepressible R. was up early, and the first in the field. After prying open his left eye, which bore the marks of yesterday's conflict with the stumps, R. takes the wash-basin and repairs to the kitchen, (he was a great favourite with all the help), and begs from them a dozen or so of eggs and some milk, goes to **the bar,** and with liquor, nutmeg, sugar, &c., makes his wash-basin full of a compound he called his " Oil of Gladness," with which he repaired to the doors of the sleeping apartments of all his commercial friends. " Here, heave out old fellows, heave out. There's a balm for every wound—try a dose of my 'oil of gladness.'" To sleep was impossible with him kicking and shouting at the door, so we tumble out and let him in with his big dish and table-spoon ten of which constituted a dose, not so bad to take either. Away he goes to "the next lucky man," until he went the rounds, and all were served alike. He finds his way to the bar-room, where, if there chance to be any agricultural gentlemen, and they are sure to be up the first in the house, warming their boots by the fire, R. serves them with a dose to cheer their hearts, by telling them that clothing is to be cheaper, than ever, and wheat is sure to **be a** high price next fall. After breakfast R., with **a** weak-kneed brother, are arm and arm doing the town, interspersing the calls they make with a drink at each of the hotels, not forgetting **an** occasional stanza of Rule Britania.

Selling clothing is slow work in comparison with this, and sample cases remain piled up in the hall of the hotel, where they remain until the boat commences running. R. decides to make his trip up to the landing and do Owen Sound on his return. All are glad to see him on the boat, as he is well-known to all, as well he might be, as I guess R—— clothed the principal part of deck hands, and several half-breeds thrown in. Now would be a good time to *brace up* and sober off; but this is not R's. line. In his outfit he has provided himself with the *needful*, and continues the same old drunk for the round trip, thus it was one trip after another until the house found out that his " usefulnes was gone," and replaced him. We could relate incidents in this connection of many of our old travellers, that time has weeded out from among us, that would almost be incredible. But we prefer burying them, as many of the originators of them are buried, and will close this unpleasant part of our duty by offering some advice which experience of commercial men, and their customs dictate, more especially to the young men in whom we feel a very kindly interest. Could you have the writer's knowledge of sprees and their consequences, you would neglect no safeguards that would prevent any chance of your going and doing likewise. **We advise** :

1st.—Never to drink spirituous liquors during business hours.

2nd.—Refuse to gamble or toss in any game of chance for drinks.

3rd.—Be particular about your friendships—choose the companionship of the **temperate.**

4th.—Strike up no impulsive friendship with men of whose habits you know nothing.

5th—Be punctual and prompt in all your habits and business transactions.

6th.—Lastly, let this be your golden rule. Be firm in your good resolutions, never wavering for a moment against your good judgment and better thoughts.

If reciting these adventures will be the means of preventing one young man from wrecking his hopes and prospects on the shoals and sunken reefs of intemperance, we will feel amply repaid, and we are sure all who have brothers, fathers or husbands, commercial travellers will say with the old gray haired gentleman who was making a speech at the opening of a very elegant, costly and commodious temperance hall in England : "That if the money expended in the erection of this massive pile of beautiful architecture would only be the means of saving one young man, he would feel that it was money well expended." Some one interrupting said, "it would be a very expensive outlay for one." The old gentleman, with tears streaming from his eyes, said, "No, not if that *one* were my son;" and so we all feel that if we could say anything or do anything that would be the means of saving *one*, especially if that one was *ours*, we would not lament the cost.

Young commercials, and all other young men, the play may be a bright and dazzling one while it lasts, but you must face the hard sternness of the world at last, and your jolly good spree may end you in ruin, utter and complete.

Let us have enjoyments by all means; pleasures are eminently right and proper. But a good time is not secured by a headache that lasts all the next day. The simplest pleasures are always the most lasting. In all your travels and all your knocking about nothing will obliterate the remembrances of those twenty-five cent pic-nics you had when a young fellow, when you chatted nonsense with the girl you loved, and all the other girls too, and laughed the good old ringing laugh of innocence and boyhood. No, commercial, the good time that you could not take your wife and sister to, that you would lie about, rather than let your mother know of; the memory of *this* class of good times will *never* come back to gladden and refresh your heart, as that twenty-five cent pic-nic. The good time that wakes in the morning and wonders when it was and who saw it, and when all the money is gone out of your pants' pocket. The good time that toils itself off with a headache, there's precious little fun in that, and it will only take a little fun of that kind to embitter and poison the memory of your commercial travelling days. The sting is the smallest part of the bee, but when you pick him up by it you would be apt to think that the rest of him was as large as an elephant. Yet would this little sting outweigh in your remembrance all the good, sweet, harmless, honey-ladened propensities of the bee. Let us have our enjoyments by all means; enjoyments which are hearty, ennobling and refreshing; avoid all others, *especially* the jolly good spree, which does us no good, reflects dishonour upon us, gets us into disrepute with our employers, loses us the confidence of the men we do business with, and alienates us from the affections of those we love and who love us; ruin our health, and, what is of more importance, the immortal interests of our souls.

## THE RELIGIOUS COMMERCIAL.

This is a class of commercials of which we have very few to boast of. I regret to say that the proportion is very small, not more than one in fifty, I fear. There are many of us moral, and pretty good living fellows, but few, I fear, thoroughly changed men, and when we look the matter fairly in the face, it causes us some surprise, for, as a rule, commercial men are thinking, intelligent men, and look well to their own interests, as well as their employers. But this, *the one thing needful*, and the thing of most importance to all, is neglected. Why it should be so, is surprising. When any worldly interests are at stake they are quickly on the alert, and "leave no stone unturned" that will accomplish their end. A train was about to leave London station, when a lady suddenly exclaimed, "I have lost my ticket!" Her concern became so great that the passengers all interested themselves in the search, to endeavour, if possible, to find it, but in vain. The ticket could not be found. You will be led to remark that it is not very strange that fellow passengers would interest themselves in the search, and each show anxiety to find it. They were anxious for what did not concern them personally at all, it was only the passport, "good for one day only," for that particular person, and would soon be forgotten. But this other is a matter which concerns every man, having a ticket or passport good for life, and the Life that is to come, which a great many have not got, yet to be had for the acceptance, and yet how few seem concerned about the trip, whether they are provided with a ticket or not. It is a journey we all have to take, and woe be to those who are not provided with a passport.

You may see a man buy an insurance ticket and post it to his friends, and look as if he had done a very prudent thing. It is a very strange thing we see men who are so thoughtful and prudent about the present, yet have no thought of the future, which is of such vital importance to them, and careless about insuring eternal life. We respect and warmly admire the moral courage of the religious commercial, who bends his head in reverence to invoke Divine blessing on his food, if at an hotel table, surrounded by the gay and thoughtless. I tell you it requires more pluck and moral courage to brave public opinion than to face a cannon ball. The latter can be bought for money, but the former can only emanate from a good resolute and courageous heart. Let us, therefore, ask our brethren to respect the religion of our good men. Go on, religious commercial, example is bettter than precept. "Cast thy bread upon the waters" by your good example, it may find its way to some thoughtless heart. Your quiet example may influence a thousand times more than you have any idea of. It may induce a train of thought, commencing with the bright innocent days of our boyhood in the old home, where we first bent the knee in prayer, and continue working in our minds, until a change is wrought. Our business, as you know, swarms with temptations of nearly every kind, and then there is no kind mother, or sister, or faithful wife at hand, no warning friend to encourage us in resisting it. On the contrary, there are lots of so-called friends, who pronounce you a "jolly good fellow," because you are not what you ought to be, a *religious commercial*.

### THE INDUSTRIOUS, SUCCESSFUL COMMERCIAL.

These are the men who come to the front, boys. These are the men who will succeed to the business of their present employers. In fact, we have plenty of instances of this among our wholesale merchants of the present day, which should be an incentive to make all travellers industrious and consequently successful. "Industry will bring with it its own reward"—a reward that the industrious deserve. Good positions, good salaries, the good opinion of their employers, their customers, and their fellow commercials. For who can help but admire the industrious commercial. You will find him up early in the morning, with samples all arranged, breakfast over, and ready for business by the time the shutters are off. No late breakfasts, long smokes, or toasting his toes over the fire for him. That will do for the lazy. He sticks to his customers, pleads eloquently, and uses persuasive logic, trots up and down all day, never seeming to tire, carries his own samples. He scarcely finds time for dinner, and, wet or dry, he pegs along industriously all day, gradually removing prejudice, and winning his way into the good graces of men who, perhaps, otherwise would not have anything to do with the house he represents,

He works hard until six or seven. Has he done, then? Oh, dear, no! He, perchance, has another customer coming in, or has to pack his samples to be in readiness to get on to the next town, or has to write out the orders he has booked during the day. After finishing these duties you will find him steer off to bed, as he knows he has another day's work on hand to-morrow, and good rest is needed—rest of body and rest of mind. He knows he has to throw his whole force into the work to be a success. In the old time success might have been won by the man who gave but a thimbleful of brains to his work, but in these days of close and keen competition, it demands the closest application of the whole thinking faculty, as well as the muscles, to attain success. The writer is of opinion that successful travellers are not duly appreciated by their employers. If some such men as the writer knows, who have made nearly all the trade and connection which their firm enjoys, (putting some one else's nose out of joint in order to do it), were connected with American wholesale houses, they would, before growing gray-headed, and spending the best portion of their lives in roughing it and fighting the battles, have been rewarded by an acknowledgment in the way of a junior partnership—for who has a greater claim?

When we think of a man leaving family, home and friends, for weeks at a time, roughing it in all kinds of weather, putting up with inconveniences and discomforts, laying himself liable to catch all sorts of diseases, and taking the chances of having his precious neck broken any day of the week, besides abusing his health by dissipation, irregular meals and sleep, and perhaps forming habits that like letters cut in the bark of a young tree, grow and widen until he cannot master them, spending, perhaps, a good portion of his earnings to make and win friends and customers. One is not surprised if at the end of ten years he has made a lot of money for the house he represents, but precious little for himself. Then who should reward him but those he made money for? But, as a rule, they do not. We hope the day will come when industrious and successful Commercial Travellers will hold their connection with such a firm grip, and their customers stick so close to them, that they will be able to command their price, and receive that attention and consideration that they well deserve, and wholesale houses be forced to recognize their influence and importance in connection with their business, thus deservedly rewarding the class of travellers who are *industrious and successful.*

## CHAPTER II.

### WHAT A COMMERCIAL TRAVELLER SHOULD BE.

What a traveller should be—Good Appearance—Good Manners—Good Natured—Eloquent—Enthusiastic—Pluck—Endurance—Self Reliance Punctuality—Diligence—A **Little** Assurance—Truthful—Decision—Energy—Caution Policy—Perseverance—Attention to detail—Quickness and Rapidity—Steadiness—Honorable—Good judge of character—Self Respect—Able to **pocket Affronts**—Must Excel—Loving and Religious.

WE will endeavour, from our experience, to give what we consider the qualities of an ideal "Commercial." But as Archibald Forbes says of his war correspondent, "I fear such a man never was, nor will such a man ever be." However, the following qualities should be among the many others essential in the make up of the successful "Commercial."

### GOOD APPEARANCE.

The appearance of the traveller goes a long way to determine what kind of a man he is himself, and to a certain extent most business men assess the value and standing of the firm by their traveller's appearance. A seedy suit of clothes, a shabby hat, a dirty paper collar and soiled shirt-front does not as a rule advance you in the estimation of business men, and may lose you an order, as the critic judges that you travel for an unimportant firm, who can't afford to pay you sufficiently well to enable you to appear as you ought. There is hardly any career in which an ill-favoured countenance is not a stumbling block at the outset that may never be surmounted. Especially is this the case with the Commercial Traveller.

### GOOD MANNERS.

Manner is "all in all" whate'er it be. The bearing of a man towards his fellow men, oftentimes more than any other circumstance, promotes or obstructs his advancement or success in his calling. The human mind is susceptible to flattery, and a kind manner will win us before we are aware of it. As the rough and uncultivated baggageman said of the writer, on introducing him to his friend (we had always treated him kindly and courteously), "this gentleman got right inside of me quicker than any man I ever met." With a stranger a good manner is the best letter of recommendation. A vast deal depends upon first impressions, and these are favourable or unfavourable, according to your manner. Gentleness, courtesy and refinement open all hearts to us, while coarseness and awkwardness repel us and close the avenues of approach to our friendship. Emerson says, "Give your boy accomplishments and a good address and manners, and you give him the mastery of palaces and fortunes. Wherever he goes he has not the trouble of earning them or owning them; they solicit him to enter and possess." Chesterfield wrote to his son, "You had better return a dropped fan genteely than give a thousand pounds awkwardly, and you had better refuse a favour gracefully than grant it clumsily." It is said of the Duke of Marlborough, "that his charming manner often changed an enemy into a friend," and that to be denied a favour by him was more pleasing than to receive one from another man. Mathews says, "What a man says and does is often an uncertain test of what he is, and it is the way he says and does it that furnishes the best index of his character." Polite manners are defined as benevolence in all things. A true gentleman is recognized by his regard for the rights and feelings of others. In company he is quiet, easy, unobtrusive, putting on no airs, never hinting by word or manner that he deems himself better, wiser or richer, than any one about him. He never boasts of his achievements, or fishes for compliments by affecting to underrate what he has done. He prefers to act rather than to talk, and above all things is to be distinguished by his deep insight and sympathy, his quick perception of and prompt attention to, those little and apparently insignificant things, that may cause pleasure or pain to others. Frankness and cordiality mark all his intercourse with his fellows, and however high his station the humblest man feels instantly at ease in his presence. Almost every one of us can recall a number of cases within our own knowledge, when pleasing manners and kind attention have made the fortunes of lawyers, doctors, merchants, and men in all walks of life. Few persons have influenced more powerfully the persons with whom they have come in contact than Bishop Fenelon. The secret of his sway over hearts, was his uniform courtesy, a politeness springing from a profound love of his fellow beings. Lord Peterborough said, "He was a delicious man, and that he had to run away from him to prevent his making him a Christian." If manner and courtesy lead to such consequences, is it not folly to despise or neglect it? Should not the cultivation of it be an important part of every man's education? Let me advise you strongly to be good natured and mannerly to all, whether customers, fellow commercials, or the servants who attend to your wants at hotels. There is nothing to lose and everything to gain by such a course.

### GOOD NATURE

Is one of the successful man's best aids in business. It is especially requisite to the Commercial man. You will meet buyers who would try the temper of an angel, but you will be master of the field if you can assert your superiority in good nature. A man will win his way to an order by good nature where it could not have been taken in any other way, for if the buyer be ever so business-like, an ill natured traveller has no charm for him. A happy disposition and good nature makes a host of friends for the possessor, and all vote him a "jolly good fellow." He is welcomed wherever he goes, and even if old, solemn, business-like dry bones is morose, his good nature will warm him up, perhaps convulse him with laughter, and he succumbs; in fact, you laugh him out of an order. Remember, there is nothing lost by good nature, boys.

## ELOQUENCE.

An oily tongue is persuasive, and some lines of samples, and the firms that they represent, require a good deal of oil to smooth over their inequalities and imperfections. It is but natural that men yield more readily to the active than to the passive claim upon them. Says Matthews: "A barking dog is more useful than a sleeping lion." Blow your own trumpet if you do not wish to be trampled under foot in the rush of competitive strife, and die in obscurity. Sound your charge and ride over somebody, or somebody will sound his charge and ride over you. Look at our politicians. Is it not those who sound their horn that reach the treasury benches? With a confident blow and a throng of words they carry the day with the multitude. How the coy country maid is fascinated with the eloquence of her city lover, when perhaps her neighbour's son, who is more deserving but lacks eloquence to express his admiration, is left in the shade.

## ENTHUSIASM.

If you would succeed as a traveller, you must give your whole heart and mind to your work. The man who toils without heart cannot hope for the success that attends one who strikes with all his might. Ardour and earnestness make a man's blows tell. It is not talents or acquirements altogether, but enthusiasm and energy that win the battles in life. There never was a time perhaps, in the commercial struggle, when high success demanded harder or more incessant labour or enthusiasm than now. A burning enthusiasm is needed in every one who would succeed. It is the lack of this that accounts for the non-success of men in all the walks of life. If we work up enthusiasm in our own business, we endow our customers with the same feeling. "Mocking is catching." So is enthusiasm. We *must* command the admiration and attention of others, if we hoist our flag of enthusiasm. Hoist it boys! Stand to it and all your good principles.

## PLUCK.

Battles have been won against large odds, simply by the pluck displayed by the contestants. The superiority which pluck gives to a few men over a great number was vividly illustrated by an incident which occurred a few years ago in the town of Lynn. During a public disturbance twenty of the Boston police cowed and kept in subjection a crowd of nearly three thousand persons. The mob was led by reckless men, who appeared determined to do violence, especially to the police. With loud outcries, and armed with bricks, clubs, etc., the rioters advanced to the attack, expecting to overwhelm the little squad of their opponents at the first onset. Instead of making them quail, the only effect it had on the latter was to make them more determined to maintain peace, which duty they had been sworn in and delegated to perform. They passed fearlessly into the heat and centre of the riotous demonstration, faced the thickest of the shower of missiles, and seized the ringleaders with a grip and valour that sent a shock of trepidation into the rebellious throng. It was a trial of pluck over numbers—of a few determined and plucky men over a half hesistating rabble. How our sympathies are excited in any contest where the odds are against the "little un" who enters the fray, because he had the pluck to do so; do we not always wish to see him win? And why? Simply because we admire his pluck. McLaughlin Bros., of Montreal, one of the largest and most successful dry goods firms of this day say, "We were never afraid of failure, and we would sooner have failed than not be among the greatest." It is the pluck, this bull-dog tenacity of aim and purpose, and stubbornness of perseverance which win the battles in life, whether fought on the field or in the mart. Hundreds of men go to their graves in obscurity who do so because they lack the pluck to make a stubborn fight. Sydney Smith says: "In order to do anything in this world that is worth doing we must not stand shivering on the bank and thinking of the cold and danger, but jump in and scramble through the best we can." It is better to have the pluck to decide wrongly occasionally, than to be forever hesitating and wavering. The poet Holmes says :—

> "Be firm, one constant element of luck
> Is genuine, solid, old Teutonic pluck.
> Stick to your aim: the mongrel's hold will slip,
> But only crowbars loose the bulldog's grip;
> Small though he looks, the jaw that never yields
> Drags down the bellowing monarch of the fields."

## ENDURANCE.

A traveller should be as physically perfect as possible, as he will find not only a tax on his mental, but on his physical abilities as well—this getting up sometimes before daylight to catch early trains, and turning out in the cold; this irregular taking of meals; this mixed variety in cooking them, this sleeping in different beds almost every night, sometimes on feathers, sometimes hair, sometimes straw, sometimes the soft side of a railway cushion; changes of temperature; frosty days; rainy days; buffeting with the elements; out when you should be in; the rough breath of Old Boreas sending you shivering along the street, and searching for the weak spots in your garments; days when the flood-gates of heaven seem open. You can't fill your order book toasting your toes in the snug sitting-rooms: you must turn out and "face the music," rain or shine. All these things tend to put a man in condition. There is a fierce struggle going on in all departments of trade, and the mental wear and tear is enormous. We are doing business at fever heat, and we must succumb if we are not well fortified, and have not plenty of endurance to back it up. Wholesale merchants and manufacturers require you to *grind* hard in this age. The wheel must go around with lightning rapidity, and the hours you have to turn it "on the road" are long. You will require endurance in your make-up if you pull your boat successfully to the winning-buoy. But like "our boy in blue," you must succeed if you endure to the end.

## SELF-RELIANCE.

"Self-reliance makes ability available," and it frequently leads to the possession of qualities which at first were only assumed. It is well to have the quality naturally, but if you have not got it, cultivate it. It will grow. "Help yourself and Heaven will help you." Help from within always strengthens, help from others enfeebles you, as it will tend to make you rely on others instead of on yourself. A determination to be one's own helper wins half the battle. Mathews says, "God never intended that strong, independent beings should be reared by clinging to others like the ivy to the oak for support." The difficulties, obstacles, trials and hardships to be met with on the road are positive good to some. They knit the muscles more firmly, and teach self-reliance, just as by wrestling with an athlete who is superior to us, we increase our own strength and learn the secret of his skill. You will become master of your calling by being baffled, thwarted, or checkmated by either customer, or opposition traveller. You will acquire a better knowlege of how to go about your "biz," and the next effort will be attended with increased skill and better chances of success, as it will bring out your latent powers. Swift says: "although men are accused of not knowing their own weaknesses, yet perhaps as few know their own strength." It is in men as in soils where sometimes there is a vein of gold which the owner does not know of. Your occupation will have a tendency to make you self-reliant. You will have to act often on your own judgment, in accepting or refusing offers at reduced prices for goods. You have no employers at your elbow to run to, and refer the matter. You stand by the guns yourself. The lamented Carlyle has written that, "He who has battled, were it only with poverty and hard toil, will be found stronger and more expert than he who could stay at home from the battle concealed among the provision waggons or even rest unwatchfully abiding by the stuff." In the midst of the fray of commerce you will have to defend yourself. See that you grasp your sword-hilt well and strong.

### PUNCTUALITY.

Many travellers have failed from want of punctuality. When circulars are sent out stating a day on which you are intending your visit and you fail to turn up, your customer concludes that if you are not conscientious about your appointment, you will be equally careless about your other engagements, and they will refuse to trust you in other matters. During your daily engagements great care should be taken about making your appointments, but when once made be punctual to the letter. Recklessly breaking an engagement is a waste of others time as well as your own. The successful man in every calling has a keen sense of the value of time. Nelson attributed his success to punctuality. Napoleon studied his watch always. It is related that on one occasion his Marshals, who had been invited to dine with him were ten minutes late. Rising to meet them, the Emperor, who began his dinner as the clock struck, and had finished it, said, "Gentlemen, it is now past dinner, and we will immediately proceed to business"; whereupon they were obliged to spend the afternoon planning a campaign on an empty stomach.

Washington was also rigidly punctual. It is said that when Hamilton, his Secretary, pleaded a slow watch as an excuse for being five minutes tardy, he said, "Then, sir, you must either get a new watch or I must get a new Secretary." In business this element is as important as in military matters.

A great writer says, "Punctuality is another virtue which must be cultivated by all who would succeed in any calling. It is emphatically the virtue of a mercantile and busy community. Nothing inspires confidence in a man sooner than this quality, nor is there any habit that sooner saps his reputation than that of being always behind time." Thousands have failed in life from this cause alone. Unpunctuality is not only a serious vice in itself, but it is also a parent of a large progeny of other vices. So that he who becomes its victim becomes involved in toils from which it is almost impossible to escape. It is a familiar truth that punctuality is the life of the universe. The planets keep exact time in their revolutions, each as it circles around the sun, coming in its place at the very moment it is due. So in business, punctuality is the soul of industry, without which all its wheels come to a dead stand, and you will find unless you are punctual you will come to a dead stand, so far as your success on the road is concerned.

c

## DILIGENCE.

"Time flies," and the traveller will find it flies very quickly when he is pocketing no orders. It will not do to lie in bed late, and take things easy generally, in this age of competition. Up early and up late is the motto. Unremitting application should be given to business the live-long day. All men who have made their fortunes in commerce have been pre-eminently distinguished by their intense and steady industry and application. You must like your work; in no other way can you be thoroughly diligent. It is ardour and earnestness that tell the tale in the size of your order sheets. The plodder will win against brilliant talents and ability unused. How often have we admired the traveller who, on arriving at his hotel, procures his sample room, gets his goods displayed, and is off like a shot after his customers. It will not be his fault if he does not succeed. All things being equal, he *must* succeed.

## A LITTLE ASSURANCE

is a good thing, and the traveller will find it will stand him in good stead often, especially if he is young and inexperienced. It is a fine thing to feel that you thoroughly understand your business, and that the value you are offering is unsurpassed. You can approach a buyer with that assurance which must command his attention. "The good opinion that gets abroad of us must begin at home." If a man of tolerably fair talents arrays his pretensions before us and backs them up with vigorous assertion, we are inclined to admit them even in preference to superior merits which their possessor, by never pressing them upon us, leaves unnoticed. Men are busy with their own affairs, and have no time to probe beneath your surface to find out all your good qualities, so it will not appear strange that a degree of assurance is necessary. Those who would secure our good opinion must come forward with their claims, and at least show confidence in themselves to gain ours. We are apt to forget the true merits of those who are backward by their very unobtrusiveness. Lawyers say, "Continual claims keep alive the title to an estate." A great writer says: "There is a good deal of cant about the success of forward and impudent men, while men of retiring worth are passed over with neglect. But it usually happens that these forward men have that valuable quality of promptness and activity, without which worth is mere inoperative property." In the world's busy hum an unshaken confidence in yourself and a firm conviction that you are on the right track, will do much to guarantee your success. I do not for a moment endorse the bold, forward, impudent swagger assumed by some, but trust the man of judgment to know where to draw the line.

### ABOVE ALL OTHER QUALITIES A TRAVELLER SHOULD BE TRUTHFUL.

If a man gets a reputation of perverting the truth

he had better "hang up his fiddle," as far as success on "the road" is concerned. He may commence at first with small stretchers, which he improves upon till in time stretching becomes a habit, which grows by unseen degrees until it fetters him with one of the worst of man's many vices. "Man," says Paley, "is a bundle of habits," and habit, as we all know, is a second nature. As the snow gathers together, so are our habits formed. Mathers says, " walking upon the quarter deck of a vessel, though felt at first to be intolerably confined, becomes by custom so agreeable to a sailor that in his walk on shore he often hems himself within the same bounds." Then beware of forming habits of untruthfulness. You see where it must land you, if persisted in. Samuel Smiles says: "However tolerated, lying is more or less loathsome to every pure-minded man or woman." "Lies," says Ruskin, "may be light and accidental, but they are an ugly soot from the smoke of the pit, and it is better that our hearts should be swept clean of them without our care as to which is largest or blackest." "Let him that would live well," says Plato, "attain to truth, and then, and not before, he will cease from sorrow." Outside of any future consideration, which itself is vitally important, your present prosperity depends upon your reputation for truthfulness. How often have we heard merchants pass remarks about travellers, such as "Oh, you can't believe what he says;" or, "I have found him often to tell me untruths;" or, "There is no dependence to be placed on him" etc., etc. Nice record that. Can the same success attend such a man, as **the one of whom it** might be said "**I never** knew him, in **all our business** transactions, to tell me an **untruth**. I always have the utmost confidence in what he tells me," etc. Whatever else you **do**, my man, be truthful in all your business transactions.

DECISION.

**To** decide well and promptly is often **an important** element in success.

> " Seize **the very minute,**
> What you **can do, or dream** you can begin it,
> Boldness has genius, power and magic in it,
> Only engage and then the mind grows heated,
> **Begin and then** the work will be completed."

**It has been** truly said that "**the** great **moral victories** and defeats of the world, often **turn on a minute."** It will not always **do to** be waiting **for Blucher** to **come up.** 'Twas his promptness and decision that won for him the name " Marshal Forward!" There is hardly any calling in which decision is not sometimes imperiously needed. The vacillating man no matter **what his** abilities is invariably pushed aside **by the man of** decision of character. No matter **whether** this **quality is inborn or** acquired it is **a quality** vitally important to success in the " commercial; " you will **often be called upon to** exercise it in your transactions **with** your customers. " Those who hesitate are lost." If an offer is made you for any line of goods, decide quickly and promptly what you will do, as you will then command the **situation.**

## ENERGY.

It is said that a lobster when left high and dry among the rocks has not instinct or *energy* enough to work his way back to the sea; but waits for the sea to come to him. This plan of action would not answer the Commercial Traveller. The lobster remains where he is and dies. Although the slightest effort and energy on his part would enable him to reach the waves which are perhaps tossing and rolling within a yard of him. You can't afford to wait for the wave, you must stir up the waters yourself, and manufacture the billows which are to set you afloat by your own energy. Every man who would get on, must put heart and energy into everything he does, trials or discouragements should not prevent or deter. All the world's great men who have become famous by inventions or improvements, have forced their way to distinction by energy and perseverance. "There is but one way of attaining to excellence," says Sydney Smith, "and that is hard labour," and a man who will not pay that price for distinction had better never become a Commercial Traveller.

## CAUTION.

"Proceed with caution, carrying a red signal," is the railroad man's orders. So travellers should be cautious as to what they say and do. Men's words and actions live after them, and you will find if you have been incautious, your words will live in the memory of your

## WHAT A COMMERCIAL TRAVELLER SHOULD BE.

customers to your **sorrow**. Be cautious what you say about other **merchants and other travellers**. We knew of a traveller **who** was speaking very unkindly of a brother commercial, and who after finishing what he had to say, was politely informed by the merchant that he had been speaking about his cousin. The order Mr. Traveller took that day from that merchant was "in his mind." Instances occur each day where men "put their foot in it" by being incautious. How often do we hear men say that they "have wished the earth would swallow the**m**," or that they could have **sunk through** the floor. Simply by being incautious about what they have been saying, they have been treading on the toes of somebody **who** was present. Your customer will soon find out **whether** you are cautious or not, he may confide in **you** and tell you little secrets which you incautiously **tell** someone else, they come back to his **ears and you are** "booked." You will catch a customer, who is a "tough one," quicker by caution than by incaution. It is all plain sailing when you have the power over him by a lengthened acquaintance, but **at** first you must feel your way, you must be like the cat. The eagle swoops down upon his prey, while the cat must cautiously approach and secure after patient watching.

### YOU MUST EXERCISE POLICY.

If **you** would succeed you must use a great deal of policy in your transactions with customers to keep them in good tune with the firm you represent. It would do employers much good to take the traveller's place for a trip or two and see for themselves the position the traveller is often placed in between the firm and customers. Orders not shipped in time or only partly filled; some very desirable lines sold out, attention not paid to instructions as to dating or shipping, etc.; the traveller hears of all these little irregularities on his return visit, and he has to be the go-between to heal up the breach. In fact he has to exercise as much policy to keep his list of customers complete as the leader of the Government has to conciliate and keep his following in good tune. If more policy was exercised in the counting-house and in correspondence with customers, there would be less occasion for the traveller to exercise policy. Policy is also useful in approaching one of these kind of customers, who think they know everything and a little more. A friend of ours, just having received his samples of new Spring prints, thought of having a rap at a big gun in the dry goods way in a certain town. But it would never do to go and ask him directly to buy, as he was an Importer. Our friend went in with his print samples, and said "he had just received them, and as he knew Mr. Blank was an authority, he desired his opinion on them; if he pronounced favourably Mr. Traveller could go ahead with so much more confidence in offering them." Mr. Blank, highly flattered of course, —*how easy*—opened them out, examined patterns, etc., and exclaimed, "These are right! these are right! kindly leave your cards until I look over them." Our traveller calling again, was de-

# WHAT A COMMERCILL TRAVELLER SHOULD BE. 83

lighted to find he had selected two or three hundred pieces for which he gave him the order, and was rewarded for the policy he had adopted.

The traveller on entering the customer's place of business, should be alive to all going on around him, take in the situation at a glance, say the right thing at the right time and in the right place, be sympathetic and receptive, and adjust himself to the conditions, say only that which his customer would be pleased to hear, play harmoniously upon his feelings, and put him in good humour and at ease with himself. "Talent," says a writer, "knows *what* to do, tact knows *how* to do it."

Emerson says:

> 'Tact clinches the bargain,
> Sails out of the bay,
> Gets the vote in the Senate,
> Spite of Webster or Clay."

Keep your eye on the weathercock, so that you may take advantage of every wind that blows.

## PERSEVERANCE

is indispensable, for it is the most important requisite to success on the road. Without it the traveller must take a back seat, and had better never have attempted travelling. He will find the weakest must go to the wall. Those who succeed push on firmly and bravely. The competition in every branch is so keen, that unless a man makes himself conspicuous and prominent

in his line by perseverance, he **will find that some
body**, probably less worthy than himself, **but possess-
ing more "push,"** will distance him, **and win the place
he ought** to have occupied. It is said that **you may
put a** Yankee **on** a desolate **island** in the Pacific, and
leave **him** with but a jack-knife, **and he** will get home as
soon as the vessel that left him there. **It is** spirit like
this that generates success in any calling. Perseverance
is indispensable to a successful traveller.

### ATTENTION TO DETAIL.

You must pay attention **to** detail. Here **is an** important factor. "Straws show how the wind blows," **and**
attention to little things shows the difference **between**
men **who** have succeeded and **those** who have **not**. A
great and distinguished man asserts "**that in** nine cases
out of ten, when men have failed of success, it was owing
to the neglect of little things deemed too microscopic to
need attention.

All successful **men have been remarkable** for their minute attention to details. Like the elephant, they can
move enormous masses, or pick up a pin. **In your occupation** as a traveller, if you neglect detail **and** attention to little things which some would deem too trivial to
bother about, you will soon find it will have its effect **on**
the number of your orders. Business men like attention
paid to little things. A very successful retail merchant
told me that he had built up his trade by keeping a good
stock of small wares—little things, you see!

In giving orders, pins, thread, needles, buttons, tapes, may seem small matters for you **to neglect, but the merchant** knows their value, and intrusting you to replenish his stock, **if you** neglect, you do him an injury, and yourself **no good,** as he will find some other traveller **who will** pay more attention to detail. Mathews says: "**The** difference between first and second class **work in every** department of labour, lies chiefly in **the degree of care** with which the minutiæ are executed."

**An** Eastern **merchant, who** had **amassed a large fortune,** when asked to what he attributed his successes, answered: "If **there** was any **one** thing to which, more than **to** another, **he** could attribute his wealth, it was that he **made it a point never to** neglect the details of his business." **Many men leave** the execution of small things to subordinates, **and the** result is, in the majority of cases, they are neglected, and in consequence **of** the neglect of clerk or employee, they remain at the foot of the ladder. "Small leaks sink big ships," and neglect of small duties **sinks big firms.** Let us advise you strongly **to** be most particular **about** the **details of your** work.

### QUICKNESS AND RAPIDITY

should be **a part** of your qualifications. Quickness of thought in accepting **or** declining any important point will inspire confidence **in you, by** thorough business men. They admire despatch and promptness. Rapidity of action will get you through your daily rounds, while **the slow-coach** is thinking about **it, and** you will distance your competitors. **This age of** railroads, telegraphs, telephones, **and** electric lights, has developed **quickness and** go-aheaditiveness, **and you will be left behind in** the race, unless you come up to the "scratch" promptly, and strike your best gait after getting there. You will accomplish more work, get through your trip sooner, and perhaps with more success, by adding to your other qualities rapidity.

### STEADINESS.

Steadiness amid the temptations which **are thrown** around you each day, is a virtue which the firm will seek after and appreciate in their representative. It **is as** necessary to have a clear head as an active body. You will command more respect, if your moderation **and** temperance are known facts, **even from those who dissipate themselves, and** we would **not only advise moderation** but actual prohibition as regards drinking usages, as **well as other vices to** which Commercial men are prone.

The responsibility **of a** traveller **is** great. To do justice to his employer **and to** himself requires steadiness, and he should be equal to the demand upon him, for no man can otherwise secure a place **and make a name as a** thoroughly efficient **and** reliable traveller. "Steady, boys steady."

### HONOURABLE.

**Y**ou must be honourable **in all** your transactions with your fellow-travellers, **as well as** your customers. It is of the utmost importance to have that name **among** men, and deserve it. Other travellers **can do you** either a good or bad **turn** with merchants according **to** the estimation in which you are held by them. Your name is often canvassed, unknown to you, between tra**veller** and merchant, and you get either an "Irish hoist" or are "advanced a peg" according to your deserts. The merchant will also soon find out whether you are honourable or not, "Getting the best of **him**" **won't wear, it may** do one or two trips, but if continued you will find that your "usefulness is gone." **Be** honest, be honourable, and you establish confidence with your customers which will grow in strength each succeeding trip, and your upright and honourable course will win the **golden** opinions of your fellows and success will **crown your course.**

### GOOD JUDGE OF CHARACTER.

**You** will find a mixed lot in **your** list of clients. You ought **to be a** good physiognomist, and able to dissect them. **You** will encounter all sorts of men and every imaginable kind **of** disposition coupled with all the peculiarities that flesh is heir to, and **he** who can best adapt himself to the disposition and tastes **of** his customers will find **this** accomplishment **an** invaluable aid to a full order book.

A good student **of** human nature **will be** at ease and friendly with a customer the first **trip,** when perhaps another who had called upon him **a** dozen times feels a reserve and coldness not understanding how to adapt himself. You should be able to adapt yourself to the varying dispositions, peculiarities and eccentricities of your customer. It is essential that the traveller should consider his buyer's taste first. You will always find the most successful salesmen do so. You can't afford to quarrel with the customer. That's not your "little game."

The Syndicate bargain in the recent session of Parliament, formed a topic of conversation during our last trip with nearly every customer. We are always careful what to say on this particular subject. Men are very thin skinned and very egotistical, and wait judiciously for the *cue*, which being given, we at once agree most heartily with the arguments which are advanced. Genial good humour is the result, and perhaps a good order our reward. As for instance we call upon a young, new-blown, aspiring merchant, (he has just been defeated at the Municipal elections for Councillor), he salutes us with, "Well sir, what do you think of the Syndicate bargain? Well—a—you—see—a—a—we—" "Oh, we must have the agreement entered into by the Government carried out," breaks in the young politician. "Yes, you are quite right, sir," we reply; "The salvation of the country is assured by its accomplishment," etc. The youthful Disraeli at once dubs us a "sensible fellow," and tells us that So and So called yesterday, "a pig-headed grit," but he did not give him a line, of course we got the line and are rewarded.

Then we call upon one of the old school, he is eager for the fray, and exclaims——" Well, sir, what do you think of this Syndicate bargain?" Think, sir, well you see—" " Why, sir, I ask you can any sensible man endorse so corrupt and infamous a transaction, the people surely will not submit to it." "I entirely agree with you, sir. I can't understand why they should," etc. etc. The old man rubs his hands with pleasure. "It is so delightful," he says, to meet a man who is not a fool, so many travellers are notorious Tories. Egotism on his part makes him dub us "a wise man," because we reflect his opinions. We need not tell you that we succeed with the old boy because we agree with him, which goes to prove that success is attained by studying to please.

### SELF-RESPECT.

A man cannot command the respect of others when he has no respect for himself, and here we desire to draw attention to a practice of some of our fraternity, which has a tendency to lessen the respect in which we are held by the public, by those individuals having no respect for themselves, their honour, or their word; and that is the reprehensible practice of travellers borrowing money from merchants, hotel-men, or from each other, getting merchants to back their drafts when they know they will not be honoured, getting *tick* for their hotel-bill until next trip, which said next trip is sometimes not taken, and of getting clothes, etc., on credit from merchants. We cannot too strongly denounce this business and those who practice it. Fortunately there **are** short-lived men on the road, but their evil doings live after them, and others have to suffer in their stead simply by sailing in the same ship. We would advise merchants to exercise caution in their dealings with these gentlemen, who we are pleased to say, comprise but a very small per centage **of** our craft. The fewer the better, and if we could have **our** way they would be fewer still, as we would hold up both hands to expel them from our associations. The same will apply to those who abuse the privileges in any way, so gracefully granted to us by the different lines of railroads, etc. If by applying the lash and exposing them, we could rid them out, then we have done **a** good work. We like to see men set a high value on themselves, and deserve it, we find that the world pays you about the price you ask for yourself. Travellers in oriental countries tell us, that to him who would be respected then an air of conscious importance is really necessary. The orientals, they tell **us**, have no idea it can pay to respect a man who does **not** respect himself.

### ABLE TO POCKET AFFRONTS.

For they will undoubtedly be **offered at** some time in your travels. Some men are very inconsiderate as to the feelings of others, and if you are so unfortunate **as to** represent an unpopular firm, you will get a dose **of** affronts—sometimes from men who are not any better than your firm, and not nearly so good as yourself, but you cannot afford to quarrel, even with these miserable specimens.

You must be superior to the man who forgets himself so far as to offer an ungentlemanly affront: swallow the physic, and by-and-by the sugar may come, as the fruit of your self-denial. It is a pity that we have to smother our feelings occasionally, but depend upon it, although it is a difficult thing to do sometimes, it is the best policy. You will find, with all your self-sacrifice of feelings, you will not, nor cannot, please everybody, and, if you expect to, you will be very much disappointed. If you please the majority you may feel quite satisfied, rest and be thankful. You have enlisted in the fight, you must expect to meet the foe. Be prepared, not only for the contest, but its consequences—and a part of the consequences is the impudence you will receive from cads of merchants and their supes. It would serve them right, when they offer such affronts, to treat them as Mr. C., a member of a dry-goods firm that once existed in Hamilton, treated an upstart. Mr. C. accompanied their traveller on a driving trip west, and in the course of their journey, pulled up at the door of a merchant, who was an old supply account of theirs. Entering the store while the traveller drove the horses over to the tavern, Mr. C. was accosted by a stripling of a clerk, sitting with his feet up on the stove, reading, with: "Hallo! more bummers: more bummers than customers now-a-days. We don't want to see you; you are becoming a nuisance; you need not take your samples off the waggon," etc., etc. Mr. C. stood for a moment in surprise, when he quietly reached for a bundle of cotton yarn which was on a centre table, and let fly at Mr. Clerk, knocking him over off the chair. Mr. F. the merchant, who lived in the back part of the store, hearing the confusion and noise, hastened out, and seeing Mr. C., whom he recognized at once, exclaimed: "Why, Mr. C., what is the matter?" Mr. C., says: "That puppy gave me some insolence, and I took the liberty of knocking him over." "Quite right, sir—you did quite right, sir." If more of these upstarts were served in like manner, we would have to pocket less affronts. But, boys, consider where they come from, and treat them accordingly.

### YOU MUST EXCEL.

Whatever is worth doing is worth doing well.

It is related of a celebrated Boston merchant, William Gray, that having on a certain occasion censured a mechanic for some slovenly work, the latter, who had known Mr. Gray when he was in a very humble position, bore the rebuke with impatience. "I tell you what Billy Gray, I shan't stand such words from *you;* why I recollect you when you were nothing but a drummer in a regiment." "And so I was," responded Mr. Gray; "so I was a drummer, but didn't I drum *well,* eh?—didn't I drum well."

Brougham, ranging during sixty years over the fields not only of law and politics but of science and literature, triumphed in all; and such was his love of *excellence,* so indefatigable his perseverance that it has been said if he had begun life as a shoe-black he would never have rested contented until he became the best shoe-black in England.

Socrates explained how useful and excellent a thing it was that **a man should** resolve **on** perfection in his own line, so that if a carpenter, he will be the best possible carpenter, or if a merchant the best possible merchant. It is by such means that true success is achieved. "**Such a carpenter,**" Socrates said, "would win the wreath **of carpentering,** though it was only shavings." Take the case of Wedgewood—he had the true spirit of the worker. He rose from the ranks; he looked especially to the quality of **his work, and never was satisfied until he had** done his **best. This** was the source of his power and success. If **his work** did not come up to his idea of what it should be, he would take up a stick, break the vessel, and throw it away, saying: "This won't do for Joseph Wedgewood." This is the spirit which should fill a man in his labours, and if it does, he will come to the front. Endeavour to be the best traveller in your line: do what you have to do well, and your firm will appreciate it, your customers will appreciate it, and endeavouring to do well, will, like a habit, grow upon you, and the result will be that *you will excel.*

### LOVING AND RELIGIOUS.

"**Love thy** neighbour as thyself."

"**Do unto** others as you would have others do unto you."

By following these golden rules, coupled with the foregoing qualities, **you will** be the *model* commercial man.

By loving your neighbour as yourself, all your transactions will bear the light of day. And He who seeth in secret will reward you openly. Even better be without many of the foregoing excellent qualities than be without religion.

Religion satisfies the noble wants of human nature, and intemperance, profanity, and immorality in others will be subdued by the power of religion in *your* heart. Your influence and example will have its effect, and will lessen or entirely remove in others the desire to do evil. Besides no man can prosper so well in his undertakings as when he has the Bible for his guide and God for his counseller.

## CONCLUSION OF WHAT A COMMERCIAL TRAVELLER SHOULD BE.

No one need try to become a successful Commercial Traveller who is void of originality. There is no mistake but what men are destined for particular callings. The youth that fails in one kind of business may be eminently successful in another. A young man whose bluntness was such that every effort to make any use of him in a dry goods' store was found unavailing, received a note from the principal that he would not suit, and must go. "But, I'm good for something," said he, loth to be turned into the street. "You are good for nothing as a salesman," said the principal. "I am sure I can be useful," repeated the young man. "How—tell me how?" "I don't know, sir—I don't know." "Nor do I," and the principal laughed, as he saw the eagerness of the lad displayed. "Oh, don't put me away, sir—don't put me away; try me at something besides selling. I know I cannot sell." "I know that, too; that's what is wrong." "But I can make myself useful somehow—I know I can." The blunt boy, who could not be turned into a salesman, and was so little captivating that he was nearly sent about his business, was tried at something else. He was placed in the counting house, and in a few years not only became chief cashier in the concern, but eminent as an accountant throughout the country. Some people cannot forge shapes or patterns for themselves. Their place is where they have to do a fixed amount of work for a fixed amount of salary. No originality. They won't do for travellers. Others are good imitators; but on the road there is no one to set them patterns. John Adams' father, a shoemaker, undertook to teach him the craft, gave him some uppers to cut out by a pattern that had a three-cornered hole in it to hang it up by. It was found that he had followed the pattern exactly, triangular hole and all. Besides, the borrowed talent of another is only temporary.

You must centre your mind and abilities on your calling. Your talents may be dazzling, yet if scattered on different objects, they lose their force. Michael Angelo, the great painter, was a success, because he concentrated his abilities. When asked why he did not marry, replied, "Painting is my wife, and my works are my children." Do not waste your ammunition in careless firing; if you desire **to make** a breach in the **wall**, take sure aim at the *one spot*. **If you have** only limited abilities, you have a greater need **for** effort **and** concentration.

Do not stand idly complaining **of your** abilities. **Pope** Gregory VII. **was a carpenter's son, Sextus** V. a shepherd, and **Adrian VI. a bargeman.** Copernicus was a baker's son. **An obscure monk split in** twain the Catholic Church. Clarkson, **who** killed the **slave trade** when it was at its height, was of obscure origin. Arkwright, **a** barber's apprentice, with little or no education, won for England by his wonderful mechanical genius, **what is now** considered worth **more to her** than all her possessions; and Richard Cobden, who was once **as you are,** a Commercial Traveller, by perseverance overthrew **one of** England's deep-rooted commercial systems. **There** is no telling what future greatness is in store **for you. Always remember** that it is **the** man who honors **the calling, and** conduct yourself accordingly. **If at** times you feel cast down, remember that **it is** difficulties and obstacles that make **good men. Some** flowers **need** to be crushed before they will yield their sweetest perfumes. Guard well your habits, which, **by** unseen degrees grow, and fasten themselves like ivy **to the wall.** Twist, split, prune, pull up by the **roots** all bad ones. They begin in **cobwebs, but** they end **in** chains. Let the habits that **fasten** themselves to **your** character be **those** of method, accuracy, observation, punctuality **and** despatch—cultivating those which, upon examining **yourself,** you find you require.

*Be* as you would wish to appear; always **remembering** that you belong to a class **who *are*** gentlemen. Play **your part so as to raise** the reputation of the company, and let it be said **of you when** you have passed off the st**a**ge, that there **is one** less good, brave, **true** man, who was an honour to himself, **his** fellow-man, **and his** God.

## CHAPTER III.

### OUR CUSTOMERS.

Our Customers—The Model Polite A 1 Customer—The Civil, Jolly Customer—The Punctual, Industrious and Successful Customer—The Advertizing, Go-ahead Customer—The Careful, Prudent, Cautious Customer—The Systematic Customer—The Fault-finding, Unpunctual Customer—The Incautious, Talkative Customer—The Too-knowing Customer—The Fast Customer—The Fossilized Customer—The Impudent, Bull-dog, Know-nothing Customer—Customers who are so on Suffrage.

GOD bless,—well some of them, for they are a mixed lot, and can very well stand assorting,—we will classify them as follows :

Some **A 1**, can't be better.

Some very good indeed.

Some just middling.

Some do not amount to very much.

Some that respectable commercials ought not to call upon.

Some as mean as human nature can make them.

These are sub-divided into a number of kinds.

The model, polite, and **A 1**. customer.

The civil, jolly customer.

The punctual, industrious, and successful customer.

The advertising, go ahead customer.

The careful, prudent, cautious customer.
The systematic **customer.**
The fault-finding, unpunctual customer.
The incautious, talkative customer.
**The too**-knowing customer.
The fast customer.
The fossilized customer
The impudent, bull-dog, know-nothing custome
Customers who are so on sufferage.

### THE MODEL, POLITE, A 1 CUSTOMER.

**We know of a few, but** they are **like** the religious commercial, **scarce.** We have one in our mind's eye now, he is a rare jewel, would there were **more like** him. On entering his store, if he is in his office, the moment he perceives a commercial gentleman waiting **to** see him **he** leaves his work and comes forward. **Or if he is** engaged with a customer he makes it a point **either to** finish **as** quickly as possible with them, **or spare a** moment to come forward and meet you with **a** pleasant smile, **which** affects you so agreeably that if he **does not** want to buy **a** line of goods you leave his presence **more pleased** than you would be with many half-reluctant, **uncivil** merchants, who have promised to see your samples. He either tells you that he does not think there is a single **line he** can buy from you, or else " Let me see, **I** think there are a few things we want and we will see your samples at four o'clock." When four o'clock arrives he will be there to the moment. There **is no** beating about the bush to get at him, no nonsense about how is business, how are all your able-bodied relations, what is the news, where have you been, what are the crop prospects, &c. He is business, and intends attending to it, and allow you to attend to yours, not wasting your time and his needlessly. At the same time he is polite, although it may be natural to him, he knows the value of cultivating it both towards his customers and all others. And here let me say that we know of a great many pretty decent customers who are perhaps really good men, but who could double their influence if they could contrive to be a little less stiff and more elastic, if they would but oil the rust on their manners occasionally. We read of hundreds of instances where men have made their fortunes by their politeness and civility. It was through his civility to a couple of strangers, one of them a foreigner, that Mr. Winans, of Philadelphia, is said to have obtained some years ago his invitation to go to St. Petersburg and manufacture locomotives for the Russian Czar. The gentlemen had been shown with indifference through the larger establishments, but on their coming to Mr. Winans, a third or fourth rate factory, he took so much pains to show them all its parts and workings, and was so patient in all his explanations and answers to their enquiries, that within a year he was surprised to receive an invitation to transfer his labour to Russia. He went, accumulated a large fortune, and ultimately received from his workshops in Russia a hundred thousand dollars per year, and now he has one of the largest private fortunes in Philadelphia. All this the result of his civility and politeness to strangers.

"Thank you, my dear," said Lyndefoot to a little beggar girl that bought a penny worth of snuff. "Thank you my dear, please call again," made Lyndefoot a millionaire. The model customer is not only polite to us, his customers and his help, but is punctual with us when he engages to come and see our samples. He is there on time, no ocasion going to the door and looking up street to see if you can see him coming, no anxiety about your catching the train in his case, you know he will be there and on time, and you make your calculations accordingly. He just consumes the proper time in your sample room, putting you to no unnecessary trouble, as he always knows what he wants. He never deludes you with the hope that he may order before you leave town, when he knows he has no such intentions, and keeps you in town longer than you intended, in order to tell you so. In fact the A 1 customer knows how to treat a fellowman, even if he is an A 1 and a prompt payer, well off, and lives in a large fashionable house. He knows how to treat a commercial, even if he does represent one of the smallest and most insignificant of our wholesale houses. Such customers make travelling a real pleasure, besides we believe it pays them. They are well spoken of by commercial gentlemen. Such men, A 1 model customers will be quoted at the lowest possible prices, and if the traveller has any " Plums " to offer he is sure to have the refusal of them. People as well as travellers make a note of merchants who are obliging and civil, and give them their custom in consequence, (and I tell you this is an important and successful advertisement as we carry the news). It is related of the late Mr. Butler, of Providence, that he was so courteous and obliging as to re-open his store one night solely to supply a little girl with a spool of thread which she wanted. The incident took wind, people talked about it, brought him a large run of customers, and he died a millionaire, and he deserved it. Some years ago a dry goods salesmen in a London shop had acquired such a reputation for courtesy and exhaustless patience that it was said to be impossible to provoke from him any expression of irritability or the smallest symptom of vexation. A lady of rank hearing of his wonderous equanamity, determined to put him to the test by all the annoyances by which a veteran shopper knows how to treat a shopman. She failed in the attempt and thereupon set him up in business. He rose to eminence, and the mainspring of his success was politeness. These instances show the true character of the A 1 customer, and it is surprising that there can be found any other kind, when if they only read and observe, they would see that it is not only the proper course to pursue, but brings with it its own reward, increased respect, increased business, increased wealth, and last, but not least, doing unto others as you would have others do unto yo

### THE CIVIL, JOLLY CUSTOMER.

There are a class of customers who are civil, obliging, and jolly enough, but lack what commercial men appreciate in the A 1 customer, promptness, and attention at *once* to business. Civility is certainly to a man what beauty is to a woman, and it is very agreeable to take. It is certainly a happy trait, and lends lustre to the humblest person; in fact, it is a real ornament to them. Would that there were more who wore this ornament in our business relations with them. If it is true that it costs some men a greater effort to be civil than others, let us advise such *not to count the cost*, because if a merchant expects civility from his help, and customers, and Our Boys, he should set the example, and he can then expect to be paid back in his own coin, besides, it is the duty of the upper classes and those in position, to set such example and to teach those who look up to them. In France it is said that the reason why the lower classes are so polite, is because the upper classes are polite and civil to them. Our people are astonished when they visit Paris to find men in high positions taking off their hats and bowing to persons in humble walks in life. Such example challenges the admiration, and sets people thinking, and causes them to go and do likewise. When in addition to being civil, our customer is jolly, he is still more agreeable to take, and no one can or will object to a man being jolly. The jolly customer knocks off the rough edges, pours oil on the troubled waters, and brings up the average of customers generally. It does one good to call upon him after having visited old gruffy on the opposite side of the street. He will have his reward, may he live long and die happy.

THE INDUUTRIOUS, PUNCTUAL AND SUCCESSFUL CUSTOMER.

It is said that "it is money, or rather the want of money, that makes men industrious." Still there are those who are naturally industrious, yet do not accumulate a balance at their bankers very fast. In these cases there is a screw loose somewhere. Men must not only be industrious, but must exercise intelligence, skill, energy, zeal, vigilance, frugality and self denial.

If they desire to accumulate wealth, and wealth in this country of ours is not to be despised, the way things are heading just now. Having wealth means rest when you are tired, eat when you are hungry of the choicest food, drink when you are thirsty of the most delightful beverages; the warmest, coolest and finest clothing; the grandest houses and grounds; the choicest books and pictures; the most elegant furniture and surroundings; the finest pair of horses and trap, and Mr. brass buttons to wait upon you; in fact, all comforts and blessings can be bought with money, except health and a clear conscience.

Intelligence, learning, eloquence, talents, moral worth, all must command respect, but if a man has not got gold dust with these, his chances for comfort and all the good things of this life are slim. No wonder we are all wiring in and driving at a two-forty rate to acquire wealth. It is enough to make any of us industrious. But, as I said before, we cannot be successful by industry alone. Punctuality is an important element. The successful merchant has a keen sense of the value of time; if he makes an engagement with you he is there to the minute, and he has a right to be, after making the engagement. It has been justly said, "that there is as much injustice and cruelty in destroying a man's comfort, in the five minutes you keep him waiting, as in giving him an actual blow; the only difference is one is unintentional and the other is intentional. If the work of one hour of the Commercial Traveller is encroached upon, the whole business of the day is thrown into disorder. He has his arrangements made of selling, packing, writing and catching trains, which no merchant has any right to disorder by breaking his engagements, even by five minutes.

Sir Walter Scott, when writing to a young man who had asked him his advice, says "when a regiment is under march the rear is often thrown into confusion, because the front does not move steadily and without interruption." It is the same thing with a traveller's movements. It will not do for him to be five minutes late for his train; all business should be instantly, steadily and regularly despatched. How many merchants are made bankrupts by delays in their customers punctually paying their due accounts. This should teach others a lesson. Of two merchants with equal talents, the one who saunters into his store at almost any time between eight and ten o'clock, and the other who is always behind his counter ready for business, as the clock is striking eight, which, think you, will get the most customers. We are thankful that we have some industrious, punctual customers, and now for their successes. To be successful they must know their business, **must switch** into new tracks and shape themselves to all **the new** methods. Old, never-change is nowhere in the race nowadays. Your calling is filled with **bold,** keen **men,** such as K, of London, who are perpetually **inventing new** ways of buying cheaply, attracting customers, and underselling others; they are **up to** all sorts of expedients **and** devices; they keep their **eyes** and ears open, and **mouths** too, sometimes; they mix their brains into their business, and dive into the depths; they study how they can make more profits and lessen their expenses, and make their business more productive; they stick to their own business, not mixing in politics, or seats at the council of municipal affairs. They leave this class **of** things to the **men** who do not intend to make money out of their legitimate business. The successful merchant has other fish to **fry.** He has, **or** will soon have, a surplus, and he knows enough to use it to advantage. He will take his discounts, and these **will** amount to **quite a** snug sum during the year's business. His paper if given, is pronounced fire proof and gilt edged.

### THE ADVERTISING, GO-AHEAD CUSTOMER.

They know that to get rid of their wares they must get their name into everybody's **ears** and into everybody's mouth, and they take every means to do it. They always have special leading lines, and they make **a** noise about them. They keep their eyes open **and** their wits about them. They are always glad to exchange ideas with the intelligent Commercial Traveller, and accept all hints. They keep abreast of the times, and patronize the leading public prints. They keep the bell ringing, and are alive to all that is going on around them. They anticipate the wants of the people, and adjust themselves to existing circumstances. They do not keep their gun loaded in their hands without firing occasionally, and when they do fire they hit somebody. They make their mark. Mathews puts this case well in his description of the two rival doctors, who, he says, "are equal in learning and skill, and have just begun their professional career."

Dr. Easy puts his card on his door and in the newspapers, and then sits down in his office and waits quietly for business and patients. If, fortunately, somebody is good enough to break a leg, or be seized with a cramp, at his very door, he secures a customer; otherwise he may spend years in putting knowledge into his head by study before he will put any money in his purse.

Not so with Dr. Push. He has a mean opinion of the passive system, and not only puts up a stunning brass plate on his door, but gets himself puffed in the newspapers, salaams to all the "big wigs" of the town, dresses in the height of fashion, talks learnedly of boilorygums and asphyxia, looks wise as an owl, keeps a splendid turn-out or 2-40 horse and carriage, before he has made a visit. He hires persons to startle his neighbours at midnight by the peal of his bell, is continually called out of church, and more than once has had his name shouted as being instantly wanted while attending a concert or lecture at the Academy of Music. **Instead of sitting down in his office** and dozing over Brodie or Magendie, he **scours the streets** and the whole adjoining conntry with **his carriage** daily, from morning till night, at a killing pace, **as if life and death** hung **on** his steps, and neglecting no form **of** advertising, is probably clearing two thousand dollars per year before Dr. Easy has heard the rap of his first patient. Now, of the two, Dr. Push may be the humbug; but certainly he is not the fool.

Our advertising customer will have his **spring parcel** sold, and be ready for a new lot, while his fogy **neighbour** is trying to divine why his goods are not moving off more rapidly, little thinking that the fault lies **with** himself, and not with the goods or customers. He forgets to fire his gun, and let people know **he is in the fight.** We like to see the go-ahead customer; **he** inspires us with new push. He will make his spoon **or** spoil **his horn.** The chances **are** in favor of the spoon.

### THE CAREFUL, PRUDENT, CAUTIOUS CUSTOMER.

**As a rule, they** are not **a** success. They are of the old school, and are not suited **to** this age of excitement **and** competition. They are the hardest class **of** customers to serve, and to get orders from, and when you do manage **to book** their order, there is not much satisfaction **in it. You** have **to devote** twice the amount of time **to** them that is necessary. You have **to** call **a** number of times before they decide whether **they will** buy or not. When **you** do get them into your sample room, they will inspect every line, from A to Z, before you have a line booked. They will watch you closely, to see that you put down the right quantities (which are invariably small), and see that you put down the right price for them. They give you a most careful and guarded order, swallowing up an immense amount of your time for their poverty-stricken order. They forget that time is money, and that every minute of your time is valuable to you. They seem to forget that you have other customers to call upon and transact business with, and that you did not come to their town to board by the week, and hang around for their convenience. In fact, the over-cautious customer is a man we all dread, and his name is pretty well canvassed by the commercial fraternity. He is certainly the most annoying of our buyers, and will as certainly bring punishment on his own head. He is so thoroughly disliked, that he seldom buys his goods to such good advantage as the customer that is well liked.

### THE SYSTEMATIC CUSTOMER.

There is a pleasure even in entering their shop. All that meets the eye is systemized—the arrangement of the furniture, desks, etc. The nice, well-kept appearance of their stock of goods, and all that belongs to it, their manner of transacting business with their customers, all show that there have been study and attention exercised to accomplish this end. Nothing has escaped notice; all the bearings and details have been mastered. They have found a work for every moment, and in every moment do that work.

There is no business which, if intended to be successful, which does not demand system. It binds all the parts together, and keeps the machinery running smoothly. The meanest trade requires it. By system, a good packer in a warehouse will put into a case half as much again as a bad one. Webster tells us that "method was his presiding principle," else he would never have got through with the herculean task of compiling his great dictionary. The systematic customers are doing a good work. Their example to the young men in their employ, and to all who are associated with them in business, is beneficial. Even the Commercial Traveller can derive benefit from his intercourse with them. Were system practised more by business men, there would be less worry and vexation in the business community, less cause of complaint, and many less failures.

### THE FAULT-FINDING, UNPUNCTUAL CUSTOMER.

This is one of the chaps we dread, every trip we visit him has its store of trouble for us, no end of fault-finding and complaint. The last lot of goods did not turn out right, no matter how careful we were in taking the order, and no matter how correctly executed by the house, no matter what end of trouble all have taken to please him, it is of no use. He has the same old dissatisfied story. You cannot show him any line in your samples that he has not seen previously. He is quite aware that all the articles you are selling can be purchased at a lower rate than you are offering them at. If he does inspect your samples, he will find lines that are not as good as Brown's (one of your opposition) had? "What's your price," when quoted: "Oh tone that down, it won't do for me." If he condescends to buy, he does it so ungracefully that he makes you feel miserable. His very manner is disagreeable. He will perhaps inform you that there is really not a line wanting; at the same time intending to buy; or perhaps will give you the pleasant information that he did want a few lines, but ordered them yesterday from Newman. Or he did not receive your advice note or he would have kept the line for you. Or your hour of calling upon him does not suit him. Or he cannot see your samples until some impossible period when you know you must be miles away. The fault-finding customer is usually the unpunctual one. He makes a convenience of you, knowing you are anxious to sell him, and not caring to leave town without doing so. He never bothers himself to keep track of his implied, or perhaps expressed engagement, and you have to hang around waiting his convenience, or perhaps drop in at his place of business to remind him that he had an appointment with you, at a certain hour long since past. Some trifling excuse is all the satisfaction you get, and he perhaps repeats for a second time your former experience with him. Such men ought to be avoided and brought to time, by all first-class travellers leaving town without again giving them a chance for a rehearsal of former experiences. We would like to see this class of customers taught a lesson by the travelling community. It would do them good. Or else get them out of the way so that first-class men may fill their places.

## THE INCAUTIOUS, TALKATIVE CUSTOMER.

The incautious customer does an injustice to himself as well as to the traveller. An order given at random. Oh, just send me a few of this or that. Or you know what will suit me. Travellers when given such lattitude and privilege, are apt to take advantage of sending unsaleable goods, or too large quantities of desirable goods. He gives his notes and forgets the date of maturity. He becomes offended with you on account of his own carelessness. In his shop he has ten places for the same articles. Lack of system puts his shop topography in a mix. Stock-taking is an unknown thing to him. Of course he has himself largely to blame for being victimized. He will trust any one and every one.

And the help, as a rule, become demoralized under him, helping themselves to the contents of cash-drawers and sundry small articles too numerous to mention, resulting often in bankruptcy and ruin. Our incautious customer is usuallly a talkative customer. He is ready for an argument on the weather, crops, local scandal, politics, anybody's business but his own. You cannot hurry him—he sets no value on your time ; business to him is night-mare, and he puts the things off as long as possible. He has always someting irrelevant to say. While showing him samples, he cannot resist the temptation to tell you all about something that does not interest you a bit. He is usually too confiding, and we would often like to bring him up "*with a round turn,*" as the sailors say

He does give you an order, but it is an **unsatisfactory one,** he does not do business in **a business-like** way.

There are a **class** of customers we like **a** little friendly chat with before we commence business, but after that **is** over **they commence** their business in a proper way. **All of us like the friend in a customer** who treats us and regards us as a friend rather than a mere **commercial. We** have many. With **them we** love **a** pleasant hour when business is over, **and** when we can conveniently spare it, and will always look back **in after life** to the many such pleasant reunions we have enjoyed with them. We wish to remind **our incautious** customers, that they are not our best beloved, **and can** only become such by turning **over a** new leaf.

### THE TOO KNOWING **CUSTOMER.**

There are lots of them; they know **it all; you cannot** teach them worth a cent; they seem **to** have forgotten **that a man may** go on learning for a life time; years are required to master **the** details of any trade or calling Shrewd business men confess that after twenty years of an active business life, **they** are yet **really very** ignorant of much that **pertains to** their **business;** but our **too** knowing customer **knows it all from** the commencement. **You** cannot **show them** anything that is new **to them; you** cannot give **them** any surprise parties; they are too old for the oldest **of** us. These men make a very grave mistake, and if this should meet **the** eye of any of **this** class of our customers, they will **be** wise to take heed and stop to think. Commercial travellers are a pretty well informed class of men, and there are none of us too old to learn. Travellers can often give a customer some information that would be worth money to him, but is deterred from doing so by the knowledge of the customer's weakness. Remember, Mr. Customer, you often make a mistake, and don't you forget it. We have often introduced lines of fast selling goods, which would have been a very desirable line to have secured before being all sold, our knowing customer knows they will not sell, will not suit his trade, &c., &c. On our next visit he is making anxious inquiry about them, as his customers have seen them elsewhere, and are anxious to get some. He tries to obtain them after they are all sold, and fails to do so, and his more sensible opposition, who has taken the traveller's advice and purchased them, has made money, and a good impression on the public by having the correct thing. Too knowing men do not know as much as they think they do sometimes; they forget that they are measured by other peoples half bushels; they are measured and found wanting.

### THE FAST CUSTOMER.

There are a few of this class in the trade. They are known by their dress and style, their mode of living, their habits, &c. They usually live in good style, keep a team or fast horse, play a good game of billiards, or a little draw poker occasionally, visit the racing meetings, boat races, &c., and are generally considered "sports."

We have a word to say to those boys, and they can take the hint or not, as it suits them. Some are really good fellows at heart, and we wish them well, but we can assure them that without they change their mode of life, all will not be well with them, either morally or financially. By bad habits a customer shivers his credit into fragments. Fast living, in spending more than anyone could reasonably hope the profits of a business to be, although that business yielded a good return, must end by a game of law between customer and creditor. Result, counsel and lawyers rake down a big share of the pot, making it a bad game for debtor and creditor alike. As a rule, the fast customer is what bankrupts are manufactured from. They are the last to refuse credit and the first to forget about the payment. Merchants of these times wonder how old so-and-so made his money. He does not seem to have any extra ability or business tack, but has made his pile. Would it be information for the present generation of merchants to learn that old so-and-so lived upon four or five hundred dollars per year, while their living cost three or four thousand dollars per year. The difference between these two sums for fifty years, with compound interest, is over a million dollars. Very few estimate the enormous sums to which money needlessly wasted in personal and household expenses would accumulate if saved and put at compound interest. Try it for awhile and astonish yourself at the result.

## THE FOSSILIZED CUSTOMER.

This class of customer ought to be satisfied and withdraw from the field. They are out of the fight at any rate, and why block the road to others' progress. When a man has made a competency, and borne the burden and heat of the day, and grown grey in the service, he ought to be satisfied. Besides, he occupies the place that should be occupied by the rising generation of young merchants, who are educated up to the present requirements of business men. A varied knowledge, constant watchfulness, close application, and a display of the highest ability and power of mind are the requisite ingredients in the composition of a merchant of the present day. We are battling in an age of excitement and progress, the proof of which is the change that has taken place in men's ideas with regard to mercantile education. The slow, plodding old fogy has had his day. A man, to attain eminence now, must discard the old-fashioned methods of business, stem the tide, and live abreast of the times.

Old ideas have been pushed aside. What was considered as a marvel of invention a few years ago is now superseded by other inventions still more startling. What was manufactured a few years ago by hand is now manufactured by machinery. Everything has changed, or is changing. Our method of travelling and conveyance of goods, our postal arrangements and means of ascertaining news, our mechanical devices and inventions have changed our labour duties. The systematizing and classification of duties in the mercantile community has changed the requirements in our help. Mathews very aptly puts it in this wise: "The man that insists in doing business in the old-fashioned, jog-trot, humdrum way is as much out of place as he who insists on travelling with an ox-team instead of a railway carriage, or upon getting news by the old stage coach instead of by the lightning telegraph."

### THE IMPUDENT, BULL-DOG, KNOW-NOTHING CUSTOMER.

There are a few of this class in the commercial community, and it is our desire to hit them hard. For our own part, when we meet a man of this stamp one call suffices us. We do not want to do business with him; we shun him for the future, and avoid him as we would pitch. He ought to be doing business in the oil or mining regions, or among the half-breed Indians. Civilization is lost upon him. You can detect him the moment you enter his store or place of business. His appearance, his manner, his surroundings, all indicate the man. You approach him. Oh, how you feel your humiliating position. He is the great I am, and he knows it; his first look crushes you. You address him concerning your business! Well, he *may* condescend to answer you. If he does, what a crusher. No matter how high you hold your head he will lower it. He is as good to the irrepressible commercial as a dose of hotel clerk is to the agriculturist, with his hair full of hay-seed, who registers at a first-class hotel. "No, sir; *I* do not want anything in your line," he manages to grunt out. The traveller cannot well back out without making another effort, and dashes at him again with a few quotations that ought to stagger him. But this is no go. *He* can buy at better prices than that, or perhaps he will claim that he can buy goods at as low prices as the house the traveller represents. You are forced to take a back seat, as he holds the winning hand, and you leave him in utter disgust, mentally resolving that "you will be even with him yet," or that you will never cross his threshold again. The latter plan is, perhaps, the best. Leave the pig alone in his sty. "Live peaceably with all men, as far as in you lieth," and show such men that God has created us with equal rights and privileges, and that we can get along without him, if he can get along without us.

### CUSTOMERS WHO ARE SO ON SUFFRAGE.

This class of customer is frequently met with, but you do not meet the same one often. His is a butterfly existence. You know him for a few trips and then you know him no more. He rushes into business without knowing anything about it, and ten chances to one without capital, or, if any, very limited. Representatives of small houses anxious to do business, call upon him and he is kept supplied for a season, but his day of grace is short-lived, and the official assignee soon takes possession, and our customer drops into that obscurity from which he came. If this should meet the eye of any aspirant, let him be kindly advised to look carefully before he leaps. Things now are not as they used to be, when any one could open shop, and from force of circumstances make money. Now it is the practical, educated, industrious man, and with some capital, that has a chance of success.

Of late years we have had too many farmers, mechanics, and others rush into shop-keeping. In order to get custom they sell goods at any price, and not only do they do themselves no good, but they injure their legitimate neighbours. This is this class of customers who have supplied the country with bankrupt stocks, which in their turn have been sold at sacrifice prices, and has kept trade unsatisfactory and demoralized. From the first it is a desperate struggle with those customers to keep their heads above water, and are always trembling on the verge of bankruptcy.

They lack business talent, and providence never intended them for merchants. They try to do double the quantity of business their capital will justify. They are then on the lee shore, and cannot beat to windward, and a short time will bring them on the rocks with a crash.

## CHAPTER IV.

### OUR EMPLOYERS.

Our employers—A Word of Advice to our Employers—Employers exercising Policy.

WE would like to be able to write all we know and all we feel concerning our employers. How little do most of them know concerning the life of their travellers. Would that they could put themselves in thier places occasionally. The men we represent are as varied in kind as in business; and all kinds of business have their commercial representatives—from Allcock's fishhooks and needles to Frothingham & Workman's iron and anchors. Employers seldom properly understand the difficulties a traveller has to encounter, unless they have themselves served an apprenticeship on the road. In the counting-house it is very easy to lay down certain laws and regulations. What customers you *must* get orders from, and what prices you *must* get for goods. It is very easy to listen to, but when you come to bring them into practice how changed the scene! We find the pictures they draw are only fancy sketches. With a traveller of experience these counting-house regulations are assessed at their proper value. And whilst politely listening to these airy imaginations as to what should be done with Mr. So-and-So, we are really thinking to ourselves whether Mr. So-and-So cares to do anything **with** the house **at** all. This want of **practical knowledge as** to our calling very often produces **an** amount of instruction, which is little needed, to complicate our duties. A customer wants us **to** do **one** thing which we know can be done, if the firm chooses **to** do it. The **firm,** on the other hand, **will do** no such thing; and here we are **between** two fires. Shall we offend our customer, or **lose** prestige with the house? In this way we often **suffer very** much, and as a successful salesman, we **do not** want to do either. But one or the other must be the result. The great fault, on the part of employers, in such cases, is that instead of allowing the representative to do the best he can for them, he must be worked by strings pulled in the warehouse. The temper of the customer should be taken into account by the traveller, because this element is wanting in the warehouse, and calculations made accordingly **will** invariably be in fault.

Our employers need a word, **and a** strong one, on another subject. They seem to have an **idea that** success in business can be obtained by sending out cheap travellers, **and** cutting down expenses to the **very** lowest notch. This class of employers have their reward in due time by **a** loss **of** trade which they might have had with better and **more** experienced travellers. Their representatives are also treated meanly by other travellers, since they can-

H

not afford to do as others do. **The** reputation of **the** house is also lowered through the country by cheap travellers, as their opponents talk them down, and I don't know but what they deserve it.

Pick a good man to bear your standard in the commercial warfare; pay him fairly, send him out creditably, **treat** him respectfully, trust him implicitly, criticize him leniently, and you will find that these are principles which tend to advance your own interests as well as his. You will then, as you deserve, have success; and your business arms will stretch out, embracing all the length and breadth of the land.

Although most travellers are but employed, they feel and sympathize with employers in all the details of their business, especially in any misfortune which they have had some share in producing. There is a want of sympathy between the "road" and the counting-house, and employers would find it to their interests to look sharply **into** the matter. More trouble is occasioned the traveller **by** bookkeepers and their subs. writing uncalled for and sometimes impudent letters **to** customers than obtaining orders. The traveller has to face all this music and listen to grievances and complaints emanating from the office hands. A part of the traveller's time is occupied in smoothing over and conciliating customers who ought to be kept in good tune and favor by kind and considerate treatment from office hands. A little practical experience on the road would do office hands a world of good, and benefit both employer and traveller. It would be apt to tone down their temper, **chase away their uncharitableness,** sweeten their sour natures, and make them more tolerant of men who have shortcomings and duties of no ordinary kind to **perform, who** cannot be guided **by** mathematical exactness, nor by any fast and hard **lines, as their** policy and actions have to be as varied as the stores they **enter.** Some employers seem to think **that** if they keep constantly snarling at and spurring **up their** travellers, and keeping them in perpetual **fear of** being discharged, they will increase their exertions and **double** their orders. This is a blunder. There is not a more independent class of men in existence. **They** hold the trade **of** this country in their own hands, which some **employers have** learned to their cost, when their old travellers **have** started in business for themselves or transferred their services to a rival firm, then they find that they take the cream of the trade, and leave them the skim milk; besides a thousand minor influences that they can exert on friends and customers. These dissatisfied employers are themselves the most miserable of wretches; they grind the salaries down, and drive hard bargains with **the very** men with whom they should be most liberal. **They will** find in the end that a hard bargain is ever a **bad bargain** for the apparent gainer. Exercise a liberal and whole-souled policy toward your men. Always keep in mind that their gain is your gain. Treat your men well, and they will appreciate you, and **work** hard for you. Treat him like a dog, and he may bite back.

Some wholesale men seem to exercise the **policy** that

money-getting is the chief end of man, and as long as their bank account is increasing, **other people's** needs and **welfare** are lost sight of. Their passion for gold will and **does** starve their other affections. They will almost **live meanly and** coarsely if they can add stock to stock. **Go on.** Mortgage **yourself,** soul **and** body, to gold dollars. **Drag your** manhood down, and bankrupt your spiritual **and** intellectual faculties. **Keep** your employees' heads under water and their noses to the grindstone. No matter if their big families are wanting necessaries. **You are** getting rich. **The** successes of the selfish are far **more** wonderful than those of the generous.

A certain wholesale merchant drew the attention of **the** writer to an employee of his who had grown grey in his employ, **and** yet he was bragging that he had this man's services for **one** dollar per day. We remarked **that he** ought to be ashamed **to** say it. This same **merchant** swore in court that he **was worth over a million** dollars. **Oh,** contemptible meanness! You will **get your** reward. You may **have** a brass button chap **to attend** you **in this world, but** your attendant may be of another description in the next. Meanness in all its forms is despicable; especially is it **so** when exercised toward **those** who **help you** make your money; and in any business **matters, you** who are practising it are laboring under **a delusion.**

The "liberal soul it shall grow fat." There is no such reward promised the mean soul. **Men** will be judged according to the deeds done in their bodies, and if grinding one's help, both physically and financially, is among the ist of bad deeds, there are some men that I know who will have a long score to settle. Merchants have themselves largely to blame when they are victimized. Some seem to calculate with the greatest nicety the smallest pittance on which an employee can keep from starving, and then wonder that in accepting such a situation he should have calculated in making up the balance of fair wages from pickings. One would expect a liberal policy to employees from " men who have the vast energies to gather and distribute the products of almost every clime," condensing in their warehouse the four quarters of the globe. Many employers are up to the mark, good men and true, and not only of good principles, but good heart and sense. We have experienced both kinds. The mean ones will put on the shoe themselves. Dexterity and cunning, siding with prevailing opinions, more than intellectual endowments, win for them their place in the commercial community. The verdict of employees for these men is: Do what you may; work early, work late, sick or well; break yourself down; no thanks, no gratitude, no respect. You have had your day, you have played your tune, you have fired your last shot, and have dropped into the breach, fallen in an unworthy cause. There are plenty of others to be had when you drop into obscurity, and an early grave. You have worked too hard and too long to win a success for others' profit, and your overtasked body and brain has lost its power. Your only satisfaction is that you have done your duty.

There are employers who are men of talent, who have invincible determination, are strong-willed and plucky, indefatigable, and have an honest purpose, and know how to appreciate worth and industry, and they will show it by giving their men a word of encouragement and a fitting remuneration. For this class it is a real pleasure to work, and they should have the pick of our boys with their other help; and I will suggest for their benefit that they take advantage of the following description of the difference in travellers that are representing houses on the road. I have had an opportunity of seeing a great many travellers, and I have noticed two classes. One comes into your store, dressed like a business man, and when he finds you are at leisure, introduces himself, and you make up your mind, after talking with him, if in need of anything in his line, to look at his samples. When you do, his prices and goods please you, and when through, you find quite a list of goods you have selected. This same man comes regularly, is *always* pleasant, whether you purchase or not, and soon you find your account with the house he represents is quite large, and you ask yourself why it is? Because they send a gentleman to solicit your trade—one you can rely on what he says. His judgment is beneficial to you in buying. In fact he is a splendid fellow, and when you have a large bill to purchase you wait for him. On the other hand, just as good a house sends out an inferior man to represent them. One who comes in with a swagger, hands out his card, commences to tell you about a great time he had drinking champagne last evening with so and so. And if he attempts to talk business, the chances are he is trying to flirt with some lady just come in to purchase. You are disgusted, and tell him nothing is wanted, and out he goes. This is the class of commercials who lower the standard of men who travel and *are* gentlemen.

Merchants who send out representatives should select as good a man to represent their interests on the road as fills the most important position in the house. You will thereby do more business, and make fewer poor accounts. Have nothing to do with these giddy, light-headed youths who spend a part of their time in fooling and flirting, and disgracing by their conduct a body of men who, as a whole, are industrious, courteous and intelligent, and who for nobleness of character, will compare with the picked men of our land.

Another important matter for employers to consider seriously, is keeping, if possible, old, true and experienced travellers on the same ground. The advantage will be seen from what I am about to relate, and shrewd employers will take a note of it.

Men form acquaintances and friendships which, in most cases, are continued during their natural life. Customers like the travellers, and travellers like the customers, and many a good sale is made for the employer on personal friendship, which would never have been effected otherwise.

A certain fancy goods house in the jumping jack and notion line employs a well-known, genial, jolly good fellow whom we will call Johnny **Ferns**. Johnny represents them in the west and north, and is very much appreciated by his customers, his "moss-back" friends and the commercial community generally. Said house has a customer who was made **one** for them by Johnny's efforts, and he had **never** visited the market, and knew nothing of the firm personally. **But** he **and** Johnny were great friends. Johnny was taken ill, and was unable to make his usual trip. So it was decided that one of the partners take a run out in his stead. Reaching the town where said customer **lives,** calling upon him, and introducing **himself and** the house, Mac. says:

"Dear me—whatever! you told me **so!** Dear, now, to goodness! What **has become** of Meser Ferns, your traveller! **Dear me, he was** nice **young** man, indeed, whatever!"

"Sorry **to** say, he **is very** ill at present, **and I have** been sent to see you in his place."

"**Now,** you told me so, indeed."

"Yes; and **I will be** very pleased to take your order for **any** goods you may require."

"She'l was not able to give you order, indeed, **whatever.** I was never give any order except to the young man what calls on me pefore, you **see.** Yes, indeed."

"Oh, but you'll get the same sort of goods, you know, as I am for the same house."

"Can't **tell that,** you see, whatever. **You** was not the **same** man, indeed."

" I know that, very well. But I can sell you the same goods, and at the same prices."

" She'l not buy anysing, anyway, whatever, until she'l see Meser Ferns."

" But I am one of the firm, myself."

" She'l don't care for that, indeed. She'l know Meser Ferns was nice man, whatever, and it'll jist wait for her to come again, whatever."

With all his persuasive powers, and notwithstanding his being one of the proprietors, he could not induce Mac. to buy.

But when Johnny got better, and went to see Mac. he got a hearty reception and a good order, "*whatever.*"

## CHAPTER V.

### THE HOTELS.

The Hotels—Our Homes when away from Home—The Home-like, Good Hotel—The Pretty Fair Hotel—The Very Indifferent Hotel—The Decidedly Bad Hotel.

OUR homes when away from home. They are more varied in kind and quality than their guests are. We have experienced in our fourteen years travelling a variety that will not be met with again in this country, as we are pleased to admit that a great improvement has, and is taking place, in our hotels. But the old stager commercial will, in the good old days of teaming through the backwoods section of our country, remember the old log taverns, containing perhaps, bar, kitchen, and dining-room in one apartment, and climbing up a ladder, find the sleeping apartment providing accommodation in one room for all the guests, and the host's family. Fried pork, boiled potatoes and home-made bread comprised the " bill of fare," not forgetting the strong cup of green tea, with, perhaps, a little black molasses as a dessert. The host's wife at one of these way-side taverns was noted for the strength of her tea, and upon one occasion a traveller remarked to her that it was pretty strong, she replied, " When I make tea I make tea, and when I make water I make water." These good people always gave you what they had, with all their heart, and do their utmost to make you happy and comfortable, which is more than we can say about some of our modern hotels. It is surprising how patronising and condescending they are at some of our first-class hotels. One I could mention in particular, where they seem to act as if it were a compliment to allow you to stay with them.

You do not feel at home. You are remaining there on suffrage, although you pay for it. There is one first class hotel which I must do the justice to mention in order, if possible, to induce other first-class hotels to go and do likewise. That hotel is the Rossin House, Toronto.

Entering this hotel, you meet at the office counter something exceptional in the way of hotel clerks; and while speaking of hotel clerks, you must excuse my diverging to give a description of the hotel clerk of the present day. Mr. Diamond Pin, as a rule, is the concentrated embodiment of dignity. Perhaps you do not see what I am driving at. To experience, just go and ask one of these bed-room potentates of the wherabouts of some friend of yours who may be an inmate of the house.

Words fail to convey any idea of the way in which you will be crushed. Not that these great men are rude. Oh, no! But there is a majesty, a loftiness, an exaltation, a consciousness of position and power in their words, looks and gestures, which reduce the inquirer, in his own estimation, to the verge of inferiority. Christians who are always striving to humble and abase themselves—whose besetting sin is pride, just take a dose or two of hotel clerk. Whenever I feel that I need taking down a peg or two, and that I am getting too big for my clothes, I have a never-failing remedy. I merely step into a first-class hotel, and approach Mr. Diamond Pin, and ask, " Is Mr. Smith stopping here?" The great man, after four or five minutes, lifts his eyes, he speaks. I am crushed. But you do not find this kind of clerk at the Rossin House. There, at the counter you meet with the genial host himself, or if any of his office clerks, the impression is the same—a sense of Well, I am at home here; or, at any rate, I am welcome. No respecter of persons there; the same courtesy extended to all, whether you ask for a cheap room or an expensive one. You are not measured by the number of your dollars, or the amount of wine you are likely to buy, but you are treated as a guest. The Prince of hotel men, Mr. Irish, understands human nature and the wants of man, both physical and mental. You are pleased with him and his officers. You are pleased that you came. You are pleased that you have been well received. You are pleased with the appearance of things around you. You are pleased at the attention shown you, and when you are assigned to your room, you are pleased to find everything there that can contribute to your comfort during your stay—everything in keeping and in order. On repairing to the office counter, if you desire any information or advice it is cheerfully and kindly given you, and pains taken to give any directions that would be of use to you during your stay in the city.

The bar, the reading and reception rooms, the elevator, the closets, are all well appointed, scrupulously clean, well ventilated, and well attended. The handsome corridors, the lofty ceilings, the spacious halls, pleasant reception rooms and handsome parlors are all in keeping with each other, and remind one of the largest and best appointed of the modern hotels in the United States, where all that wealth and skill can do are brought into use in order to accomplish the grandest results. The dining room is, *par excellence*, the room of the house, both as regards size, appearance and appointments. Here the attendance is all that can be desired, and it does one good to enter the room at meal hour; every one seems to be in the height of enjoyment. Friend Irish understands human weaknesses and caters so sumptuously and bountifully, and provides such rare delicacies and appetizing viands that one cannot help pitching into them with a gusto seldom enjoyed or acquired. The cooking and preparing of all the food and eatables must be accomplished by the most experienced and skilled artizans, as everything is brought to table in such elegant taste and form that the most unreasonable connoisseur must be pleased. Every dish is a pleasant surprise, both in quantity, quality and flavor, and no one can rise from the table of the Rossin House without feeling that he is a richer, wiser and happier man, which reminds me of asking an agricultural merchant friend of mine where he sojourned when in Toronto. His reply: "At the Rossin House, of course; and do you know," said he, "after I stay there a day or two, when I return home I think myself of more importance and feel richer and happier and altogether better for having been there." This is every one's experience, or at least should be.

Would that we could say as much for the majority of the hotels we put up at in our business perambulations through the country. They will have to be classified as follows: Some are homelike and good; some pretty fair; the majority very indifferent; and a few decidedly bad.

The good, homelike hotel is where we like to make our long stays; and it is where those of us who do not go home make for to spend our Sundays. We have often ran past a town to reach a good hotel and remain over night, and return the next day, finishing it as quickly as possible, to avoid making any extended stay at its uncomfortable hotel. At the good, homelike hotel, everything is as you would like it to be: a good, well-ventilated and aired bed-chamber, with a comfortable and clean bed; a well-laid, clean, and well provided table, the food cooked well and arranged tastefully, the attendance good, and the room cheerful and well lighted. The office well-appointed, and the attendance in keeping; good, well-lighted, and clean sample rooms, with plenty of table accommodation, and a good porter to look after your traps. The closets are kept scrupulously clean; they are accessible, and provided with all requirements; and last, but not least, the new departure of a commercial room, which we all appreciate, must become an institution in hotels which desire to secure the commercial trade, and all praise is due to those who have taken the initiative in this matter. Allow me to suggest here the importance of properly furnishing and catering to the craft in this room. We need comfortable chairs in which to rest and read after the struggles of the day are over. We need comfortable and separate writing desks on which to write our orders and correspondence. These should be provided with ink and pens, blotting-pad, and mucilage bottle, and a ball of twine. Also, blank forms for telegraphing. On the walls of the room all the time tables of the different railroads should be nicely framed and hung. The room should be well lighted day and night, and kept comfortable in heat and cold, and I am sure any commercial will gladly assist by his patronage any hotel which is properly kept, and whose proprietor has had the enterprise to attend to the wants of travellers, and add an institution which has been a long-felt want.

We scarcely expect to find this and other accommodations of the good hotel at the hotel which we will call

### PRETTY FAIR.

A little improvement and a little pains taken in the keeping and management of this hotel, would bring it up to the mark. But there is something wanting about this class of house, which makes you feel that it could be improved upon. However, it is an improvement on the class of hotel which we have to describe as being

## VERY INDIFFERENT

In them there seems to be no proper head or front, no system or order, and things are decidedly mixed from the time you arrive until you leave. You will likely have to look after your own sample room, and perhaps assist in handling your baggage, and attend to other little wants. As Friend Ansley says: "There is nothing first class except the charges." But even this class of hotel is to be desired in preference to the one that is

## DECIDEDEY BAD.

They can scarcely claim the modern title of hotel. The old familiar name of tavern would apply better, and some of them do not deserve that. Some hotel men keep their hotels, others let the hotel keep them. These decidedly bad hotels should be exterminated; they are not fit for man or beast. The building itself will be found to be unkempt, and out of repair. The outbuildings, tumble-down and dirty, especially the water closet (which very necessary convenience is much at fault in nearly all of our hotels, good, bad and indifferent), and I want to be frank and fearless about this affair, no matter who gets hurt. I have no sympathy with sentimental squeamishness, which would cover up what ought to be revealed. In my experience, which covers fifteen years, this, above all else, has been the greatest annoyance to the travelling community. What should be a place of cleanliness and comfort is usually filthy and uncomfortable. Sometimes situated where you have to climb over piles of rubbish, etc., to reach it, or in some out of the way, unsuitable place, where all your movements can be observed by the inmates of the house. It is a crying shame that this state of things still exists. Our associations and papers should agitate this subject until a reformation is brought about. In the decidedly bad hotel, everything is in keeping with its name. The food badly cooked and badly served; the dining-room cheerless and untidy; the sample room unclean and furnished with broken-down tables and chairs; your bedchamber a 7 x 9 room, unventilated and cheerless, scarcely large enough to turn around in; the bed as hard as a pavement, not the kind of thing to rest weary and aching limbs on. Clothes by no means too abundant in winter time. Towel, ten inches by fourteen, pretty well riddled with holes. Soap so hard as never to be able to reach the lather in it, and the same cake greeting you on your return visit, as it never wears out. Carpet and rugs which seemed to have served other generations. It is true, at some of these houses the charges are low; but the accommodation matches the lowness of the charges to the end of the chapter. Let those hotels that are not up to the mark learn that what we want on the road, and all are willing to pay for, is a bed like what we get at the Kerby House, Brantford, on which we can sleep luxuriously, in a comfortable room, which contains every element for a peaceful sleep. A table well provided, and the food well cooked. A good cook is worth a mint of money to any hotel, as a man's stomach is a great weakness with him, and he will put up with a good deal else if he has it well filled, and enjoys the process. How few understand the art of making food agreeable to the palate. These few possess something wonderful in the way of ingenuity. They can convert a dinner-table into a picture, a literal bed of roses, serve up food in a hundred different ways, manufacture little dishes to tempt the epicure to eat, and the unfortunate without an appetite to make a trial. How different the same dishes (so-called) come on the table at the different hotels. If it were not for the name, you would not recognize them. We do not expect the same variety at every country hotel that we get at the Rossin House. Give us good food, properly cooked and served, and there will be no complaint. Now, then, give us a good, large, well-lighted, comfortable room, in which to show our samples, for the proper display of these often leads to an order. In fact, we would like to see, in the hotel business, that the gold and silver of them will gradually gain on the brass and iron, and all wheel softly into line, and try and make our homes *pro tem.* Real Homes.

## CHAPTER VI.

### THE RAILROADS.

#### Concerning Conductors.

IT will be seen from our avocation that we spend a good portion of our time "riding on the rail." It is here the traveller, who is of an observing turn of mind, has an opportunity of observing human nature, and a part of our education is made up from these experiences. Books and teachers are well in their places, but contact with your fellow passengers going through this world knocks off the rough edges and polishes to smoothness the rough places on the surface. All sorts of people, and on all kinds of errands and business, are met with at the railroad depots and on the cars. At the station, a father leaving home, perhaps for the first time, has the wife and family down to see him off. See the surprised excitement exhibited by the little ones as the train approaches. It is an important event with them. What if something should happen to the train on which he is to leave them, tears dim their eyes as the thought seems to pass through their minds, and as each in turn receives the good-bye kiss. In another group there is another kind of excitement. A newly married couple is the centre of attraction to their friends; they are about to take their first trip as man and wife. See how she has decorated herself for the occasion. How animated all seem—present joy and future—well, we cannot tell. Another group at the forward part of the train; all seem sad and melancholy, and no wonder, a coffin stands upon the truck ready for shipment. Its occupant is about to take his last ride. Here comes the hotel bus, with its passengers, and as they bundle out upon the platform, each with his gripsack in hand, it is evident they intend journeying. Amongst the number the commercial is easily distinguished; no hurry or excitement about his actions; he quietly looks after his traps and is ready to get on board. The train arrives and the excitement is at its height. Persons arriving are met by friends with their hearty shake hands and embraces. Those going are saying their last good bye and getting their farewell kisses. *All aboard* is heard, bustling and confusion is now in order, and the train moves off. Those that remain turn their steps towards home, some with happy and some with sad hearts. Those who are on board have something else to do, securing seats and arranging their traps. They have an opportunity of observing their fellow passengers, and here is presented the opportunity for the commercial to study human nature. In almost each seat a different character presents itself, each of which is perhaps worthy of observation.

# THE RAILROADS.

Our system of railroads is most complete and exhaustive. By them we are enabled to reach almost any point, many of which a few years ago were inaccessible to the commercial. What a wonderful change in our mode of travelling this has wrought. Ox teams are almost unknown; horses are kept for working or pleasure purposes; steamboats are being converted into barges for the transportation of freight, and the railroad engine now rushes by the crumbling banks of canals, once regarded as a wonder, and sounds its shrill whistle, as if proclaiming its victory at the onward march of progress, civilization and science. The same shrill whistle has startled in their retreat the wild beasts and birds of our forests and plains, forcing them to abandon their old haunts and seek security where, in a few years, they will again be alarmed by the constant and onward march of civilization, and its accompanying mighty institutions, until at length our railroads, like a network, will encircle and entwine in its mighty embrace all parts of our land. At the present time the system and its accommodations are almost perfect. The passenger coaches with their comfortable cushioned seats and handsome fittings, the beautiful and well appropriated smoking cars, the dining cars, a marvel of ingenuity and convenience, and the superb and luxuriant drawing-room and sleeping coaches make travelling so comfortable and easy that many make journeys now who would otherwise remain at home. Those who avail themselves of these advantages will find in the men who officer the roads, and in all the employees and subordinates, a class of kind, intelligent, civil and painstaking men. Especially is this the case with regard to the conductors of passenger trains, who, although their duties are arduous and heavy, find time to answer all inquiries intelligently and pleasantly, and give directions and introductions to those who are unaccustomed to travel. They must be men of patience and good nature, as the demand upon their stock of it is great.

They are asked all sorts of irrevelent questions, and how to deal with all kinds of characters, some of which are enough to try the patience of better people than we see in the world. Especially is this the case on excursion days. And when men have forgotten their manliness, and loaded themselves full of that which steals away their brains, and robs them of their intellectual faculties. Conductors handle these gentry with that easy precision and despatch, that in many cases would entitle them to a vote of thanks from the other passengers. It is wonderful how conductors get through their routine of duties with such manifest ease and regularity. Nothing but good judgment, and long continued practice would enable them to do so. Did it ever strike you when making a journey, all that a conductor accomplishes in his day's work? Taking the number of the cars he has under his charge, and keeping time upon which his train is running, getting his train orders, and watching for his crossings, collecting tickets from passengers, getting on at each station, remembering the destination of each individual, answering innumerable questions, making out his reports, and sending in his tickets at the end of his run. Besides, the responsibility they assume, having in their charge the lives of hundreds of their fellow beings, which the least mistake on their part might endanger, and, perhaps, cost them their own lives. And yet these men spend many days of hard work, risking life and limb to attain this position, which, when reached, affords them a mere pittance when compared with the onerous duties they perform.

The poorest commercial representing the smallest possible concern, is better paid, has less to do and think about, and less responsibility. If the board of directors knew as much about these men as we do, they would shave down the salaries of their big officers and add it to the pay of a class of men upon whom, to a great extent, the success of their line depends. I am satisfied from the way I have heard passengers express themselves, that conductors influence, more or less, the volume of travel on their respective lines. There is no one in his position but exercises more or less influence in his walk and conversation. How much more then do men, the principal part of whose time is occupied and associated with the travelling public. Conductors are not half appreciated by the authorities. They are a class of men who would be very difficult to replace. Their knowledge can only be acquired by experience, and a long, faithful one at that.

We must not forget to give due praise to the smoked up, grim visages, blue jacket fellows who handle the throttle of the engine. All depends upon their attention to their duties and steadiness of their habits. There are examples without number of the true heroism that these men have displayed in times of danger, often sacrificing their own lives in the hope of saving the lives of others All honour to the "boys in blue." May they live long and die happy.

Our railroads do exercise a somwhat liberal policy towards Commercial Travellers; but I think it is in their own interests to do so. It is said corporations have no souls, so that their action toward us, is a matter of dollars and cents. Not that we do not appreciate their generosity and far-seeing wisdom. You will, however, find that the road exercising the broadest and most liberal policy, in this age of competative strife, will serve their own ends best, and become the most popular and successful lines, obtaining the patronage not only of the travelling public, but shippers as well. Kindness begets kindness, and railway companies will find that the more liberal and considerate they are with the Commercial Travellers the more the Commercial Travellers (who are one of the biggest kinds of advertising mediums) will do for them in the way of influencing shipments and business generally. Hoping the railway authorities will bear this in mind in all their dealings with us, and continue not only our present privileges but increase, in so far as they can, a policy which will lead to good results for all concerned.

## CHAPTER VII.

### CONCLUSION.

THROUGH improving odd moments, while waiting on trains, etc., I have been enabled to put together the preceding chapters. And I now wish to say a few words in conclusion. Above all else, I hope that all who read what has been written will derive some benefit from it. It will repay me well if such be the result. It has been my desire to show the different kinds of travellers' their faults and imperfections, and to give all travellers my idea of what they should be; to show our customers what they are, may, or might be; our employers where they might benefit themselves and us; and our hotels how they might make us more comfortable and benefit themselves.

The *improvidence* of many of our travellers is a point I wish to touch upon in these concluding lines. No man has a right, when in health, to live so that if sickness comes he may at any moment become a burden to his friends. On the contrary, he should always be making some provision for old age. An old man poor suggests the suspicion that his life has been a failure, and he has not lived as he ought to have lived. With travellers the temptation to spend is great. Supplied with a liberal allowance of money for expenses, part of which is supposed to be spent and given away, money becomes to travellers, as perhaps with no other class of the community, little valued. Twenty cents a day spent for cigars, (and this is a small allowance), with accumulated interest in fifty years amounts to twenty thousand dollars. Whew! who would have thought you could have puffed this much money out of your mouth. If a traveller would only save one hundred dollars per year it would amount in twenty years to seven thousand seven hundred dollars, and in forty years to fifteen thousand four hundred dollars. Just think of that. Let me advise all travellers to commence to save, if they have not already done so. Do not despise small savings, if you cannot do better. It is said there is no point more important in the history of a man than his first savings. It will lead to habits of economy and system. Wellington kept an exact account of all moneys he received and paid. Washington was not a small man, and yet he kept an exact account of his household expenses, and scrutinized the smallest items. The secret of England's greatness *is her savings*. Resolve, *now*, to save. Whatever you spend now, resolve to spend less, and save the difference. You will find poverty a great enemy to happiness. It makes some virtues impracticable, and others very difficult. It will lower your head and self-respect, and place you at the mercy of others. No wonder people say they can tell a traveller at first sight, who is so completely at ease anywhere and everywhere; who dresses so well, and spends his cash so freely. Boys keep your cash to pay legitimate expenses. Do not throw your dollars away foolishly, better send them to the little woman at home, who is, perhaps, planning how to get new clothes for the children, or renew her own, and who serves you twelve months in the year, and has to remain at home for her recreation, while you ransack the entire country for yours. Exercise a little self-denial for her sake, She will appreciate any little personal sacrifice you make on her behalf. She ought to be chancellor of your exchequer. She finds every week a month while you are away, and there is not much pleasure for her until her lord returns to her. Journey after journey you are kept from her side. See the patience she manifests. She thinks of the last happy meeting, and looks forward to the next. Those on the road who are inclined to extravagance find plenty of encouragement. This title of being a jolly good fellow is very dearly purchased. You will always find plenty to award it to you, while you are recklessly spending your money treating them, who, when your money is all gone, will be the first to turn their backs upon you. You will find your best earthly friend is your own purse. Ask the friend who has received most favors from you to lend you a dollar when you are on the spree. Mark the change in his features; not like when you were asking him to drink. See the wide berth he will give you afterwards. Boys, real friendship is a fine metal, and like all precious ones, very little of it in circulation, and the share you get is small,

Be a man, demand respect, and you will get it You are placed under the influence of other men, but it is for yourself to decide whether you will rule or be ruled by them. Show the right spirit, and you will triumph. Like cork, you may be put under, but you cannot be kept under. If you are eager to work and have the power to do so, with a fair intellect, you cannot be surpassed. Do not wait for something to turn up, but *make* something turn up. Not only strike when the iron is hot, but strike it until it becomes hot. Do not waste valuable time in deploring your luck; tighten up your belt, and go after success, and you will overtake it. Success lies in being alive to what is alive around you. Adjust yourself to its conditions. Do and say the right thing at the right time and place. You cannot reach the goal without first passing over the intermediate ground, and not then without making an effort. Be strong-willed, plucky, indefatigable and invincible. Fix your purpose well and fast, and then victory or failure. Others will find it useless to struggle against you if you show the spirit of never yielding. If you wish to attain excellence, there is only one way to do it, that is, by hard labor. And if you will not pay that price for distinction, better throw up the sponge at once. Hard labor is the price of all high excellence. Get your foot firmly planted on the lowest rung of the ladder, climb steadily, one rung at a time. If you make a slip, hang on, and try and regain lost ground, not by a single bound, but by steady, patient climbing. If you want a good opinion to get abroad of yourself it must begin at home.

Be a man amongst men in the true sense of the term. Boys, look up; never look down; the old sailors tell the young ones. Hold your head high, and do nothing to lower it. Walk uprightly, in the consciousness that you are one of God's creatures, and that His eyes are always upon you. Hope on, hope ever. Hold your ground, and work hard to reach higher ground. Push as you would in a crowd to get into a gate all are trying to enter. Give your energies to the highest employment of which your nature is capable. Be alive, be patient, watch opportunities, work hard, be rigidly honest. Keep your conscience clear, hope for the best, and if you fail to reach the summit of your ambition, which is sometimes impossible in spite of the utmost effort, you will die with the consciousness of having done your best, and gained the approval of your Father in Heaven, who will say: "Well done, good and faithful servant, enter thou into the joy of thy Lord." So mote it be.

THE END.

www.ingramcontent.com/pod-product-compliance
Lightning Source LLC
Chambersburg PA
CBHW030348170426
43202CB00010B/1289